LGBT Diver
and Inclusic
Early Years Education

Children and families come in all shapes and sizes, as do members of staff. *LGBT Diversity and Inclusion in Early Years Education* will support practitioners in thinking about LGBT issues in relation to their early years practice.

It examines the history of equalities legislation and the diversity of LGBT families, alongside giving pragmatic advice to ensure that all children, families and staff feel welcomed and celebrated in the early years setting.

This book offers realistic advice and practical guidance, which result from years of first-hand experience in the early years sector. The chapters explore key topics such as:

- a brief history of legislation in the UK in regard to LGBT diversity

- good practice with children and families

- LGBT diversity in an early years work environment

- resourcing for equality.

Including case studies, reading lists and links to useful websites and organisations, this book will be valuable reading for all early years practitioners and students who want to promote an inclusive environment for the children in their care.

Deborah Price is a senior lecturer at the University of Brighton and an associate lecturer at the Open University, UK. She has worked in early and primary years as a teacher, trainer, inspector and lecturer.

Kath Tayler has worked in early years for over 30 years as a nursery nurse, primary teacher and lecturer in early years education and care. Kath is currently a senior lecturer at Brighton University and an associate lecturer at the Open University, UK.

LGBT Diversity and Inclusion in Early Years Education

Deborah Price and Kath Tayler

Routledge
Taylor & Francis Group
LONDON AND NEW YORK

First published 2015
by Routledge
2 Park Square, Milton Park, Abingdon, Oxon OX14 4RN

and by Routledge
711 Third Avenue, New York, NY 10017

Routledge is an imprint of the Taylor & Francis Group, an informa business

British Library Cataloguing in Publication Data
A catalogue record for this book is available from the British
Library

Library of Congress Cataloging in Publication Data
Price, Deborah
  LGBT diversity and inclusion in early years education / Deborah
Price and Kath Tayler.
    pages cm
  Includes index.
  1. Homosexuality and education.   2. Sexual minorities—Study
and teaching (Early childhood)   3. Sexual orientation—Study
and teaching (Early childhood)   I. Tayler, Kath.   II. Title.
  LC192.6.P75 2015
  371.826'6—dc23   2014046583

ISBN: 978-1-138-81409-7 (hbk)
ISBN: 978-1-138-81410-3 (pbk)
ISBN: 978-1-315-74773-6 (ebk)

Typeset in Optima
by Keystroke, Station Road, Codsall, Wolverhampton

MIX
Paper from
responsible sources
FSC   FSC® C013056
www.fsc.org

Printed and bound in Great Britain by
TJ International Ltd, Padstow, Cornwall

We dedicate this book to our inspirational families in all their diversity, and particularly to Maria, Elena, Marijke and Annie.

Contents

Acknowledgements

Central to this book, particularly the case studies, are all the children, families, practitioners and students we have worked with over many years. We are enormously grateful to them for sharing their stories. We would specifically like to thank Melissa Leach and Jennifer Watson from Phoenix Nursery in Brighton, who helped us think about good practice in working with children and families. We are indebted to Stonewall, who helped and advised with the legal background and whose website and publications have supported us throughout the book.

Additional grateful thanks to Fen Coles from Letterbox Library, who has supported and advised us throughout. Similarly, thanks to Clair Barnard from the Early Childhood Project, Brighton and Judy Simon for consenting to be interviewed and being so positive about this project. We make special mention to Vicky Bear and Alex Paterson who shared their experiences with us. We would also like to thank Sara Browne for her helpful comments and Shoshana Davidson for her thought-provoking blog and the interesting interview. Thanks also to colleagues in the University of Brighton who have been supportive about LGBT diversity.

Grateful acknowledgement is made to the author for permission to use her poem 'Dziecko Child' from *Syrena* by Maria Jastrzebska (Redbeck Press, 2004). Grateful acknowledgement is also made to Becky for the permission to use her poem 'My mums are getting married' (unpublished).

Finally we would like to give our thanks to Annamarie Kino and Routledge, who had the confidence and insight to take this book forward to publication.

Introduction

This book is about families. Our aim is to think about including the needs of every child. We want that to be the starting point to any thinking, conversations, planning or training that you carry out when using this book. The main underpinning question that we are fundamentally asking you is, 'How do you include and support all of the families, children and workers in your setting?' We are asking you this in connection with your current thinking about LGBT issues in regard to the children, families and workers who come into contact with your setting.

We are aware that looking at this question through the lens of LGBT diversity is a challenging task for some practitioners, but if you are overwhelmed or confused at any point by the material in this book, then we ask you to return to the vision statement that is the core ethos of our writing and at the heart of our writing; we want to enable you to support the children, families and workers in your setting as fully as you can.

> LGBT issues have no relevance in my setting because I work with little children. These things should only be discussed when children reach secondary school, if at all.
>
> (nursery practitioner)

We have both heard this many times in connection with this aspect of diversity and we want to make it clear that in this context in talking about sexuality we are not talking about sex. We are also not talking about having involved conversations with children under five about the sexual choices that same sex and transgender people make. What we are talking about is:

- supporting those members of staff who choose to share their sexuality status at work

- supporting families of children who attend the setting when their parents have chosen to share their sexuality status with the setting

- supporting children who we know have parents who are same sex or transgender

- ensuring a supportive and inclusive environment for all of those staff and family members who have chosen to share or not to share their sexuality status

- ensuring a safe, supportive and inclusive environment for all of the children who are cared for in the setting in recognition of the sexuality that they will develop

- fulfilling the legal obligation of the setting to promote good inclusive practice in terms of LGBT diversity as they would do with any form of diversity from the main makeup of the setting.

Questions about sexuality

There are some very big issues involved when talking about LGBT diversity, and this book is not the place to discuss some of these in great detail. Here we are only looking at LGBT issues where they touch on early years work. We hope to be able to signpost you to further wider reading and research if you want to explore further. In most cases, Stonewall (2014) is the best starting point for any additional reading. Some of the more general questions you might be asking yourself at the end of this book are:

- To what extent do people choose their sexuality and are some people born with their sexual preference irrevocably set? Can this change?

- Why do some people feel that they are born in the wrong body, and what makes them want to change?

- Can we influence children in their sexuality? At what age are children aware of their own sexuality?

- What does being gay mean?

These are all challenging agendas to discuss and think about further. This book is about those people who have defined their sexuality, either workers in the setting or parents who use the setting, and positive images and ethos that show children that families and people of all kinds are respected and considered valid.

We will try and not confuse the issue by looking at gender when it is unconnected with sexuality. This will be difficult, as the two may be entwined either in reality or in the minds of those who are dealing with issues.

Gender

Society can be very binary in its outlook and there is a pervading need to categorise people into male and female. In addition to this, many people hold fixed ideas about what characterises men and women – for example, what physical appearance they should have, what behaviour they should adopt, what jobs they can do, what clothes they should wear.

There are people who do not fit into those categories. Some of them will feel that they want to wholly adopt the behaviours and physical characteristics of the 'opposite sex'. Some of them will just want to explore some of the behaviours of the 'opposite sex'. Some of them will be sexually and emotionally attracted to their own sex.

What we are saying is that a boy or a girl who likes to play with toys or wear clothes that society associates with the 'opposite' sex will not automatically grow up to be attracted to their own gender or want to take this further and completely change genders. There is more exploration of this in Chapter 2.

We have endeavoured to present as broad a mix of case studies as we can. Some of those are real incidents and some of them will have a kernel of reality in them but be structured to make a specific point. We have anonymised them except when we have permission from the person involved. We hope that by doing this we have found at least one situation that will resonate with the reader. Where we have included sections from Ofsted reports, we haven't named the setting in order to retain confidentiality.

Training

In Chapter 6 we include material to support leaders and managers of settings. We assume that when we are talking about training, practitioners have already thought about the good communication and assertiveness skills they would need in order to deliver this training. These are underpinning attributes that will be needed when training such a sensitive and potentially challenging subject, and we would advise anyone attempting to introduce the activities and discussions that we suggest to a staff team to ensure that they feel confident in dealing with difficult conversations and conflict.

When in doubt, we would advise settings to seek a specialist trainer in LGBT issues. These can be found through Stonewall (2014) or from a Local Authority.

Language and terms

We would encourage you to continue your reading of this book with Chapter 2, as it provides a crucial centre to the book in terms of defining concepts and ideas. Chapter 2 also provides a useful glossary to some of the terms we use in the book that describe LGBT diversity so that you have a clear understanding of their meaning. In connection with this we would advise any setting to think about the language that they use in terms of LGBT diversity and use appropriate resources and organisations (like Stonewall) in order to keep up to date with terms used. This is no different from other areas of diversity, for example, special needs. The terms used to refer to children with special needs have changed over the years and certain words or expressions that were acceptable 20 years ago have now been rethought and are not appropriate today. This is usually because people with special needs have been involved in defining terms and have been consulted. This is the same case with LGBT and the collection of language and terms that are used when referring to this aspect of diversity.

There are many disparaging terms that are used around LGBT diversity; again, this is no different to special needs or cultural difference. Stonewall provide some interesting resources and ideas on how to tackle and think about the use of the word 'gay' in the playground or staffroom as a negative expression. This would be an interesting and challenging way to start some discussion in a staff meeting around the use and misuse of language and terms. We have chosen to use 'LGBT' in this book to express a willingness to think about a wide definition of the lesbian, gay, bisexual and trans community while at the same time root it within the realms of practitioners' experience in early years settings. We have tried to ensure that the case studies and examples that we use in this book reflect the breadth of diversity there is when talking about LGBT issues.

Chapter breakdown

Apart from Chapters 1 and 2, this may not be a book that you read from start to finish in order. We have arranged it in an order that makes sense to us, but it may be that you choose the chapter that has most relevance to your setting at this time. For this reason we include here a short summary of each chapter.

Chapter 2 – What's it all about?

This chapter gives an outline of some of the underpinning concepts and theory that the book will cover. It examines pivotal questions such as: What is a child? What does it mean to be LGBT? It also looks at the question of identity and aspects of stereotyping and discrimination in terms of LGBT diversity. The section mentioned above on language is also included here.

Chapter 3 – The legal background

This chapter looks in detail at the pieces of legislation that specifically relate to early years settings in terms of general equality issues and how aspects of LGBT diversity are included within them. It also gives a concise guide to some of the other key pieces of legislation that have affected the LGBT community. The chapter covers legislation that affects children and also the legal obligations of the settings' employment practices.

Chapter 4 – We are family

This chapter starts with the child as its centre and examines family structures in connection with LGBT diversity. We look at some similar issues in Chapter 6, but here we are very much focused on the child. Because children should be at the centre of practice, and remembering that the Children Act refers to the child's needs as 'paramount', we want to reflect this by having this chapter first rather than start with the adults and work down. We look at all the different ways that people can have children in their lives, whether or not they are a biological parent. It also looks at the different types of family groupings with LGBT parents to which a setting might offer childcare and education. It examines good practice in this context and thinks about the implications that supporting LGBT diversity can have on a setting's practice. It is important to note that we try to avoid the use of the phrase 'LGBT families' as the children are included in describing a 'family' and they may or may not define themselves as LGBT, so this term is not the most accurate way to describe such families.

Chapter 5 – Thinking about practice with children and families

This chapter extends the issues raised in Chapter 4 and looks at a wider context of good practice in supporting diversity and how this can be extended to include families with LGBT parents. This chapter firmly puts LGBT diversity within the context of good equalities practice that should be a key element of every outstanding setting. In this book we include pointers towards good practice in every chapter. This chapter really focuses on giving some key ideas for settings to include LGBT diversity in their work with children and families.

Chapter 6 – LGBT diversity within a staff team

This chapter looks at LGBT diversity in terms of staff and the setting's obligations in supporting members of staff who define as LGBT. Beyond that, it looks at providing a generally inclusive and supportive environment so that those staff members who choose not to share their LGBT identity would still feel valued and safe. This chapter includes some ideas that would shape staff training and discussions in staff meetings. This chapter should be read in conjunction with Chapter 3, on legal issues, as there are employment rights that impact upon a setting's practice with staff who define as LGBT.

Chapter 7 – Resources

This chapter looks at the way that current resources in a setting could include items that would support and promote diversity in terms of LGBT equality as well as seeing the practitioners and their commitment to good equalities practice as the central resource. It also gives ideas and suggestions for specific issues that the setting could consider when thinking about future acquisitions.

Chapter 8 – Conclusion

We summarise the content of the book and make some general statements about the importance of LGBT diversity in the early years. We also look to the future and think about the importance of this work in terms of the young person and adult that the child will become. We also look at the international perspective and the dangers of coming out as LGBT in some countries. Finally we reflect on the way that families where individuals are LGBT can be isolated in the UK.

Last but not least . . .

Before you start to read this book, there is a key example of an immediate change that early years settings will need to make to their practice. Since 17 July 2013, same sex marriage became legal in the UK. That means that same sex couples no longer have to call the legal recognition of their union 'civil partnership', and in being called marriage it can no longer be distinguished as different from that of the marriage of a man and a woman.

Because of this change in law, practitioners can no longer assume that, when a child talks about a marriage that they have had experience of, this is between a man and a woman. Children may have this experience in a range of different ways. Their parents or a family member may have got married, or they may be taken to a wedding by their parents, or they might be a bridesmaid or pageboy. They might have just overheard someone talking about a marriage or seen one on TV. There are many ways that this can come up in the conversations that practitioners have with children. It is well established that such conversations are part of good practice, listening and speaking to children is crucial to their development, and it is important to establish good equalities practice within this listening and speaking.

Thinking about this from an adult perspective, practitioners can no longer talk about marriage in terms that solely use a man and a woman as a template for this institution. Settings may think about this and decide to shy away altogether from mentioning 'marriage' in any of the activities or resources that they provide. We think that better practice would be to embrace the new and extended diversity that 'marriage' now describes and ensure that this extension of what it can mean to be married is included in the nursery practice.

Thinking about resources in Chapter 7 shows us that it would be impossible to ensure that all mention of marriage is taken out of early years play, as play should be initiated by children and their interests and facilitated by practitioners. Experienced early years workers will know that children can always be relied on to initiate the unknown and unexpected and that one of the most exciting, and terrifying, aspects of early years work is responding to children's questions, thoughts, anxieties and general play scenarios.

One parent explained about their marriage and a nursery setting:

Our child goes to what I would call a 'traditional' nursery. The staff are quite old fashioned in their views, and I can see that in the kind of activities they offer and in the way that the nursery looks. We like it and chose it because of this environment, as it related to the way that we wanted to raise our twin daughters. The staff are all very kind and our little girls love it there. One day the nursery sent a letter home saying that they were looking at marriage as an activity and would parents send in any pictures of objects that they had to do with marriage. Well, it turned out that no other parents in the small group that one of our daughters was in were actually married, but coincidentally me and her other mum had just had a civil partnership. We sent in lots of pictures of the ceremony and party afterwards and she wore the dress that she wore for our ceremony, as she was a bridesmaid for us. It made us laugh that the nursery had to really focus on a gay marriage that day, as it was obviously something they had no experience of. The manager thanked us for sending in all of the resources and admitted that she had learnt a lot that day.

We would suggest that the first piece of staff training that you lead or the first bit of thinking that you do should be about the implications that this legal change has for your early years practice. It is a very immediate and clear change that needs to be made in early years practice and we think is a good starting point for this book.

Reference

Stonewall (2014) *Stonewall: The Lesbian, Gay and Bisexual Charity* [Online]. Available at http://www.stonewall.org.uk/ (accessed 28 August 2014).

2 What's it all about?

This chapter asks you to think about the way in which you view children. Do you see a child as vulnerable and innocent, in need of constant guidance and protection, or as powerful co-constructors of their own worlds? We suggest that how you view the child has a bearing on how you will approach the issues discussed throughout this book.

Some of the issues and ideas discussed here are thought-provoking and others will address challenges you may meet in your setting and in your practice. This chapter will help you to understand these issues and encourage you to develop the confidence to deal with them.

In order to support this, important terms that are used throughout the book are introduced and explained. Finally, some issues to think about are listed. These ideas could be used within a staff team and could be starting points for discussion.

What is a child?

This may seem a straightforward question that has a quick and easy answer, and people often feel that they can confidently state what a child is. However, once you start to consider the concept in more depth, it becomes more complicated. The United Nations Conventions on the Rights of the Child states that a child is 'every human being below the age of eighteen years' (United Nations 2014). While that might seem clear and an idea we are familiar with, it is worth considering that the age of consent for sexual acts is 16 in the UK, and the age of criminal responsibility is 10 in England and Wales, and 8 in Scotland as we write (although there is a lobby to change this to 12), so there are some complexities with this issue even from a legal perspective.

When answering the question 'What is a child?', a group of early years practitioners replied in the following ways:

- someone young or someone still growing up
- a young person needing protection
- someone learning how to live and behave
- a person we need to look after
- a young person under the age of 18 years
- an immature person who hasn't reached puberty
- a young person with their own ideas, thoughts and feelings
- a little one with much to say about life!
- a girl or a boy; someone's son or daughter
- a sponge that soaks up everything around them.

How we view a child will have a great influence on how we provide for their care and education, how we support their families, and how we build the relationships we have with those children and families and with others we work with.

If we see children as weak, vulnerable, innocent and in need of protection, we will respond differently to the issues addressed in this book than we will if we see children as powerful and competent beings with important things to tell us about their lives, their thoughts and their needs. If we see children as developing along pre-determined trajectories, we will have different expectations than if we see children as co-constructing their knowledge and relationships with peers and adults.

It is a very dominant view to see children primarily as people who have not yet become adult. In this view, 'adulthood is held to represent some kind of end point to children's journey' (James 2011: 34). This approach to understanding children and childhood is greatly influenced by developmental psychology. Developmental psychology outlines the change from child to adult and suggests that there are a set of developmental norms common to all children, biologically determined and lying within the child, waiting to unfold. Piaget, a central proponent of this view, set out to chart this development, looking for the commonalities and universalities in growth and change. Prout and James (1997) suggest that the way children speak, play or engage with others is viewed and assessed as evidence of their unfolding development.

Qvortrup describes the developmental view as an anticipatory one; the child is moving from incompetence to competence. This, he argues, is based on the idea of improvement 'as the child accomplishes the transition to her/his adult life phase' (2011: 24).

In developmental psychology, 'children' and 'the child' are synonymous, where 'the child' can represent *all* children irrespective of the culture in which the child is living. Prout and James (1997) argue that the Piagetian account of developmental stages is so firmly entrenched in Western ideology about childhood that it pervades all areas of parenting and education, and it is hard to think beyond or outside it. All early years practitioners will be familiar with child development and the constructs it provides about how we view children, how we support them, what we expect of them and what we think their next steps will be. Often referred to as 'Developmentally Appropriate Practice (DAP)', this approach can be defined as

> curriculum and pedagogy based upon agreed stages of children's development. It is a framework of principles and guidelines for best practice in the care and education of young children.
>
> (Bredekamp and Copple 1997,
> cited in Nutbrown and Clough 2013)

It is such a central part of our approach that it can seem hard, or even inappropriate, to challenge it.

The rise in the new sociology of childhood challenges the view of childhood as a biological given and sees it instead as a social construction. Children are seen as active participants in the reproduction of their culture (Corsaro 2011). Morrow argues that this paradigm shift involved 'moving on from the narrow focus of socialisation and child development (the study of what children will *become)* to a sociology that attempted to take children seriously as they experience their lives *in the here and now'* (2009: 63, emphasis in original).

Vygotskian socio-cultural theory sees the child as an active co-constructor of his or her learning and relationships. Vygotsky's theory of the Zone of Proximal Development (ZPD) particularly emphasises the role of the more able peer or adult in supporting the child's learning. Supporting a child within their ZPD recognises that, with support, a child will be able to achieve things they are not able to achieve alone and that it is within relationships that learning takes place.

Rather than seeing the child as a passive recipient of the culture they are part of, this view sees the child as actively participating in the developments and changes that take place within and between cultures (Rogoff 2003). It is important to consider the term 'culture' in its widest meaning here to include all aspects of the attitudes, customs and beliefs that a society, or group within society, may hold.

While this view is evident in current early years practice and is acknowledged in the Early Years Foundation Stage (EYFS) through the recognition of the importance of the environment and relationships, pre-determined developmental norms remain central to the current pedagogical approach.

Case study 2.1

This case study is based on interviews with two early years practitioners. The first works in a small private setting. The second works in a day care setting in a children's centre. Both interviewees had been informed about the reason for the interview and that the area to be discussed was whether views on child development had an impact on views about LGBT diversity in early years practice.

Interview 1

Kath Tayler: Do you think a robust knowledge of child development is important in your practice?

Practitioner: Yes, definitely. I really need to know the children well, what they can do and what they will do next.

KT: Can you give me an example?

P: Well, you know that a baby won't stand before it can sit, don't you? So you wouldn't encourage a baby to stand up if he or she hasn't got the strength to sit up yet.

KT: What about cognitive development or emotional development? Do you think the same applies?

P: I think that is more complicated. I know children all develop at different rates and do things at different ages, but I think the broad stages are helpful. Learning language, for example, you know they will say single words before they use sentences, even though they all do that at different ages. It helps you work out how to support them.

KT: Do you think your view on the importance of understanding child development has an impact on your thinking about how to handle the issues of LGBT equality in early years practice?

P: Not really. I would never discriminate against anyone and I don't think a good knowledge of child development is relevant to that.

KT: Do you think young children can understand about different families?

P: I think if a child has two mums or dads, that will be what is normal for them and they will understand it but I don't think other children will necessarily be able to understand it until they get a bit older. Maybe when they go to school.

Interview 2

KT: Do you think a robust knowledge of child development is important in your practice?

P: Yes, I do, but I also know that children all develop in their own ways and the way that people relate to them is just as important.

KT: Can you give me an example?

P: Well if a child is talked to, listened to, read to, sung to, they'll learn to talk in a different way to a child who doesn't have those things.

KT: Do you think your view on the importance of understanding child development has an impact on your thinking about how to handle the issues of LGBT equality in early years practice?

P: Sort of. I mean, in my setting we see relationships as the most important thing and we think we all learn from each other. We've got a little boy who has been adopted by two gay men. I've never been adopted and I grew up with a mum and a dad, so I can learn from him even though he is only 3!

KT: Do you think young children can understand about different families?

P: Definitely. Young children are so open and curious. They learn from what's around them. We talk openly about these things in my setting.

Points to consider

- What are your views on the importance of having knowledge of child development?

- How does this fit with your view about whether children are co-constructors of their relationships and learning?

- Do you think your responses to these ideas have an impact on your view about LGBT equality in early years practice?

> ### Discussion
>
> There are no right or wrong answers to these questions; they are simply things to consider as you read this book. You might, however, like to keep these ideas in mind as you read the rest of this chapter and think about the impact these ideas have on the way you think about your practice.

Why is it relevant to think about child development?

In seeing children as developing along a fixed trajectory of normally occurring milestones, we are saying that we know children, we know how they develop, we know what will happen next, we know what they can understand, we know what knowledge they are ready for and we know when and how to give them information. We are also saying that there are such things as 'norms' of development, even if we accept that there is variation in the ages at which children achieve their milestones.

By saying that we know the norms of childhood, we are also saying that there are things that lie outside this norm and by being sure that we know when children are ready to deal with certain ideas and concepts; we are also saying that we know what things are inappropriate for them to know about. Mayall (1996, cited in Robinson 2002) points out that it is adults that construct understandings of childhood, what children are and what they should know.

The idea of children having LGBT parents can be in this category of 'what children shouldn't know about' for many early years practitioners. Many people may also think that LGBT people should not work with young children and may also not want to consider the fact that some of the children in early years settings will identify as LGBT themselves during childhood and/or as adults.

Taking the view that childhood is socially constructed allows us to challenge the idea that there are aspects of diversity that are outside the knowledge that a child should possess. It also challenges practitioners to face their own discomfort about dealing with such issues. This requires courage and a willingness to reflect on some possibly strongly held views. Robinson (2002: 426) tells of a practitioner who says, 'We haven't dealt with these issues because we haven't had any gay and lesbian families in our setting. It isn't really a concern to us.' By making decisions about what aspects of diversity we share with children and what aspects we remain silent about, we have an impact on children's perception of diversity (Robinson 2002).

In this book we are asking you to see this as an aspect of diversity that is relevant to all settings, as relevant as any other aspect of equality and inclusion.

Some of the challenges might include:

- dealing with a range of parental responses to LGBT staff members who are open about their identity

- dealing with a range of parental responses to staff members they *think* may identify as LGBT

- being willing to think about the potential identities that children may be exploring in their play

- thinking about your own comfort at saying, for example, 'Sally's mummies are lesbians' instead of 'Sally has two mummies.'

- thinking about how you resource your setting so that books, puzzles, posters, etc. show a range of families.

- allowing children to use the role-play area and dressing-up clothes in ways that may not conform to stereotypes.

Terms to understand

Lesbian, gay, bisexual and transgender

First, it is important to be clear about how we define LGBT people. Wolpert explains that

A lesbian is a woman who forms her primary loving and sexual relationships with other women. A gay man is a man who forms his primary loving and sexual relationships with other men. A bisexual person forms primary loving and sexual relationships with members of either sex.

(2005: 33)

Where **lesbian, gay** and **bisexual** are understood as sexual orientations, **transgender** and **intersex** are to do with gender identity and are separate from sexual orientation. A transgender or intersex person may feel that their assigned gender (usually allocated at birth and based on external genitals) does not match their internal sense of their gender. A transgender or intersex person may identify as heterosexual, lesbian, gay or bisexual. Solomon explains:

> Though the terms get used in a variety of ways, *transgender* and its abbreviation as *trans* are the most widely accepted in the trans community. A *transman* was born female and became a man; a *transwoman* was born male and became a woman. *Intersex* describes people who are born with ambiguous genitalia or are in some other physical way both male and female from birth.
>
> (2013: 600, emphasis in original)

It is also important to recognise that, for some people, the labels attached to these sexual orientations and gender identities are limiting and inaccurate. Some people may identify as **polysexual** (attraction towards people of any sex or gender identity) or **asexual** (no attraction towards anyone) and many people now recognise sexuality as fluid and something that can change over time. For these reasons many people now use the acronym 'LGBTQ', where the 'Q' refers to 'queer' or 'questioning', 'LGBT+', where the '+' is in recognition of other sexualities and gender identities or LGBTI, where 'I' refers to those who identify as intersex.

Othering and binary thinking

While most aspects of equality and inclusion are now seen as central to early years practice, issues to do with LGBT equality are often seen as not relevant to early years settings and practitioners. By seeing these issues as outside everyday early years practice, LGBT people and their children are being **othered**, i.e. they are being seen as outside the norm, different to 'us'. We create a sense of 'us' and 'them' in our early years settings. **Othering** is a very powerful psychological mechanism by which we create a sense of belonging. By saying, 'I belong to this group,' we are also saying, 'but you don't'. Implicit in the process of othering is the idea that not only is one group or individual seen as 'other' by another group or individual, but they are also seen as inferior. By othering, we are saying not only 'we are different to you', but also 'we are better than you'.

Much of the thinking in our culture operates in this 'us and them' **binary** way. We often think in an either/or way about many issues and categorise things into opposites. Even when we don't necessarily see things as opposite, we use the terms in that way. We talk of a person seeing something in black and white; of our moods being up and down; there is night and day; good and bad; rich and poor and, of course, man and woman and gay and straight. We talk of all these things as if there is nothing in between.

There is seen to be no room for uncertainty, no subtleties to our moods, no dusk or dawn, no good bits to bad things or bad bits to good things, no variation in wealth. When these things are pointed out, it is easy to see that there are, of course, huge variations in all these things but, as Solomon points out, 'Western culture likes binaries: life feels less frightening when we can separate good and evil into tidy heaps, when we split off the mind from the body, when men are masculine and women are feminine' (2013: 599). The challenge lies in developing a willingness to see a spectrum of sexuality and gender identities. In talking about bisexuality, Epstein argues that, by being visible, people who identify as bisexual remind us that 'sexuality is not a binary between straight and gay but rather is a continuum with multiple possibilities' (2013: 135).

Stereotyping and prejudice

One of the outcomes of thinking in such a fixed way is that it can lead to **stereotyping**. When we make generalised assumptions about groups of people, we are stereotyping. Stereotyping can lead us to believe that we know someone and that we know how they will behave and what they will think and feel. It can lead us to imagine that one group of people is very different from other groups of people and that differences between people within a group are minimal. Often when we first meet someone, 'we try to put him or her into categories, which may or may not be accurate' (Pre-school Learning Alliance 2011: 16). For example, we might think that gay men and straight men are very different and that all gay men share certain characteristics. As Epstein describes,

> We assume that since we have seen some camp and witty gay men, all gay men must be like that . . . To present the message that gay men are camp and witty is to force gay men into a narrow box and to allow people to just assume they know what all gay men are like.
>
> (2013: 72)

Many of us might feel that the ideas we hold about groups of people are positive and therefore not damaging. We might, for example, think that gay men are always funny or in touch with their feelings. However, even positive stereotypes categorise people and limit our expectations about the individuality of people who identify as LGBT. Many of the representations of people who identify as LGBT on television or in books conform to these stereotypes and can make it harder for LGBT people to live outside these stereotypes and be seen and related to as individuals.

Stereotyping can also be linked to our assumptions about what is 'normal' for young children to do. Our stereotypes can lead us to believe it is 'normal' for boys to play with trains and for girls to dress up as fairies. This puts girls who play with trains or boys who dress up as fairies outside that perceived norm and problematises the child's play preferences. By holding on to this stereotyping, we are othering the play of children who don't conform to these perceived norms.

Through this process, stereotyping can lead to **prejudice**. As the word implies, prejudice is to pre-judge; to form an opinion based on pre-held beliefs or information. Blaine (2007, cited in Epstein 2013: 65) describes prejudice as 'unjustified negative judgement of an individual based on his or her social group identity'. As Epstein goes on to suggest, people who identify as LGBT experience prejudice because assumptions are made about what this means. Assumptions about what it means to be LGBT are applied to all who identify as LGBT due to their identity.

Contact between people from different groups has been shown to have a significant impact on prejudice (Understanding Prejudice 2014). Although mainly studied in relation to racism, there is no doubt that the same applies to homophobia. When equality is supported by institutional support such as legislation and societal acceptance, the impact of contact between groups is even greater. With recent changes that impact on equality for the LGBT community, the conditions have never been better for acceptance and respect to develop between the LGBT community and others.

Multiple identities

It is important to recognise that most people have **multiple identities**. You may identify as an early years practitioner, as a parent, as someone who speaks English as an additional language, as a tennis player, as a carer, as a taxi driver for your children! Some identities are a part of how we see ourselves, what interests we have, what job we do or what position we hold within our families and communities. However, some identities can lead to discrimination. Many people who identify as LGBT may also be black or from minority ethnic groups, or disabled or working class. This interplay between different forms of oppression is known as **intersectionality**.

Equally, LGBT people can be racist or sexist. As Epstein points out, 'belonging to one minority group does not necessarily make [people] understanding or accepting of all minorities' (2013: 159).

This shows how complex these issues are. You might, for example, have a child attending your setting who has two mothers. It might seem to you and other practitioners that this is the defining aspect of their identity as a family. However, for them, the most important aspect of their identity is that one of them is a full-time carer for her mother who has dementia and it may be this that they need support with. For her, this is a much more present and difficult part of her identity than being a lesbian mother.

It is important to recognise that these processes are socially constructed and lead to social exclusion. As early years practitioners, you will be aware that nobody is born with stereotypical or prejudiced ways of thinking. These ideas about ourselves and others are learned and have a huge impact on our relationship with others, our beliefs and expectations about ourselves and others and our attitudes to the people we meet.

Discrimination

When stereotyping and prejudice take place, it is easy to see how this could lead to **discrimination**. Discrimination is the unfair treatment of a person or group of people based on an aspect of their identity, whether perceived or actual. Discrimination is more than a belief, as with stereotyping and prejudice. To discriminate against an individual or group of individuals because of a group they are perceived to belong to is to turn beliefs into actions.

Homophobia and **transphobia** are particular kinds of prejudice and discrimination that apply to people who identify as LGBT. 'Homophobia is the irrational hatred, intolerance, and fear of lesbian, gay and bisexual (LGB) people' (Stonewall 2014). Wolpert adds that

> Homophobia includes social standards and norms that dictate heterosexuality as moral and normal and homosexuality as abnormal and immoral, backed up by institutional power that privileges heterosexual people and denies privilege to gay, lesbian and bisexual people.
>
> (2005: 33)

The same applies to transphobia in that it is based on irrational attitudes and feelings towards transgender people. One of the ways in which homophobia can operate that has particular relevance to this book is the fear that LGBT parents will have a negative impact on the sexuality and gender identity of the children they raise. Kane (2013) describes her research on how parents think about the gender expectations of their 3- to 5-year-old children. She explains that when the parent is lesbian or gay, they feel the extra judgment from living in a homophobic society. She quotes one lesbian mother as saying, 'I feel held up to the world to make sure that his masculinity is in check' (Kane 2006, cited in Kane 2013: 53). This can be particularly difficult, as research does show that children raised by lesbian and gay parents are more flexible in their gender roles and in their approach to sexuality (Stacey and Biblarz 2001, cited in Kane 2013). Research by Bos and Sandfort confirms this. They conclude that

> Children in lesbian families felt less parental pressure to conform to gender stereotypes, were less likely to experience their own gender as superior and were more likely to be uncertain about future heterosexual romantic involvement.
>
> (2010: 114)

While there will be people who interpret this from a homophobic point of view, it is worth considering this in the positive way in which the researchers argue it. For children to grow up with greater awareness of the options and choices open to them can only be a good thing. Švab (2007, cited in Kane 2013) argues that it is in countries where homophobia is most prevalent that lesbian and gay parents receive the greatest criticism for not raising appropriately gendered children.

Clarke, Kitzinger and Potter (2004) argue that the fact that children with lesbian and gay parents sometimes experience homophobic bullying has been used as an argument against lesbians and gay men being parents. This argument is in itself homophobic, in that it is the parenting that is criticised rather than the homophobic bullying.

The fear of and contempt for people identifying as LGBT can lead to discrimination. There is no hierarchy of discrimination. It is not a competition to find which group or individual is most damaged by discrimination. All discrimination is wrong and should be tackled. Research carried out by Stonewall (Guasp 2010) shows that children of LGBT parents feel that their schools don't treat homophobia in the same serious way as they treat other forms of discrimination. Guasp suggests that this means that children acting in a homophobic way don't learn to understand the impact that their actions can have. The children in the study said that the fact that homophobia is not dealt with makes them want to hide the truth about their families. They also said that they find the use of the word 'gay' in an insulting way very hurtful and they want to see teachers challenging this. Although this research took place in primary schools, many of the views expressed would also apply to early years settings. It is also arguable that the early years are when these views begin to form and that we have a responsibility to engage with children at an early age to help prevent later discriminatory behaviour.

Sometimes LGBT people can be so deeply affected by the discrimination they experience that they can turn it against themselves. This is known as **internalised homophobia or transphobia**. This is a very negative experience for those experiencing it and results in low self-esteem and even self-hatred (Stonewall 2014).

It is not so long ago that lesbian mothers lost custody of their children simply because of their sexuality. It is easy to see the processes discussed above in action here. By othering lesbian mothers, those responsible for making decisions about custody were able to separate these situations from generally held ideas about assessing the best interests of the child when parents separated. The binary way of thinking about things led to the view that a woman could be a mother or a lesbian, but not both. In fact, the term 'lesbian mother' was seen to be a contradiction in terms (Golombok 2002). Stereotypes of what a lesbian mother might be like led to the view that no woman identifying as a lesbian was fit to be a mother. This stereotyped view also led to the prejudiced belief that children would be psychologically damaged by being raised by a lesbian and that the children would show atypical gender development (Golombok 2003). These strongly held views led to direct discrimination towards lesbian mothers and to their children. The legally sanctioned homophobia had life-long implications for the families concerned.

Although it is now not likely that a lesbian mother would lose the legal right to parent her child through being a lesbian, many less extreme and more subtle forms of prejudice and discrimination continue to persist in many aspects of life for people who identify as LGBT.

25

Tolerance and beyond

Read any writing on equality, diversity and inclusion, and you will come across the concept of working towards a **tolerant** society. While tolerance might indicate an open and permissive attitude towards those whose opinions, race, sexuality, etc. differ from one's own, there is also an aspect of tolerance that implies endurance or putting up with something. It does indicate acceptance but not necessarily in a positive way. This needs to be considered carefully in relation to families with LGBT parents. By tolerating families with LGBT parents, we are saying there is what Short refers to as a 'family hierarchy' (2007: 59). This hierarchy would give greater status to families with a mother and father, while there would be a tolerant acceptance of other family forms. This is not good inclusive practice and does not belong in a setting committed to equality and diversity.

Although discussing this issue in relation to multicultural education Nieto (1994) argues for moving beyond tolerance and acceptance and instead engaging with the issues in order to work towards **respect** for diversity and difference. She argues that this can lead to a willingness to face the challenges that diversity can bring, and to higher levels of understanding.

Things to think about

Think about your responses to all the points below. You could use them as discussion points in the staff team in your setting.

- When thinking about the question 'What is a child', what responses did you have? Think about whether you see children as weak, vulnerable and in need of protection, or powerful, co-constructors of their own worlds.

- Do you think your understanding of child development has any impact on your willingness to engage with these issues?

- What is your response to the idea of dealing with the issues addressed in this book with the children and families you work with?

- Who do you think might be othered in your setting? Do you ever feel othered yourself? Which parents or children do you think might be being othered by your setting or by other parents or children?

- Do you find the idea of challenging binary thinking interesting? How could you approach this?

- What examples of stereotyping can you think of that apply to your setting and the way you work with children and families? You might be able to think of negative and positive stereotypes. How could you challenge these stereotypes?

- Can you think of times when stereotypes you are aware of have led to a prejudiced view of an individual or group of individuals?

- What identities can you think of in relation to yourself? What ones do you see as central to 'who you are'? What identities do you think of in relation to your colleagues and the children and families you work with? Do you think these are the same identities they would see as important for themselves?

- Are you aware of the impact that discrimination can have on people? Are you aware of any instances of homophobia or transphobia in your setting? How can you, as a team, address this?

- Do your think your approach to equality and diversity moves you beyond tolerance and allows you to think in a respectful way?

Conclusion

This chapter has asked you to think about some complex issues and has suggested that there are ways these issues can be embraced in your practice. By using the question 'What is a child?' as your starting point, you will have set the groundwork for the issues to follow. This question will have encouraged you to consider whether you see the child as the passive recipient of the knowledge and ideas you, as a practitioner, have to impart to them, or whether you see the child as an equal, a co-constructor of the learning environment of your early years setting.

Your thinking about this will have helped you to think about your approach to working with children who have LGBT parents. With this underpinning thinking, the chapter then encouraged you to consider some of the challenges you may encounter in your practice. This has been supported with some discussion of the terms you may encounter as you think about the relevant issues and ideas. You may like to return to these explanations as you read the rest of the book, as they will help your thinking and discussion.

References

Bos, H. and Sandfort, T. (2010) Children's Gender Identity in Lesbian and Heterosexual Two-Parent Families. *Sex Roles,* 62(1–2): 114–126.

Clarke, V., Kitzinger, C. and Potter, J. (2004) Kids are Just Cruel Anyway: Lesbian and Gay Parents Talk about Homophobic Bullying. *British Journal of Social Psychology,* 43: 531–550.

Corsaro, W. (2011) *The Sociology of Childhood.* London: Sage.

Epstein, B.J. (2013) *Are the Kids All Right? The Representation of LGBTQ Characters in Children's and Young Adult Lit.* Bristol: HammerOn Press.

Golombok, S. (2002) Why I Study Lesbian Mothers. *Psychologist,* 15(11): 562–563 [Online]. Available at http://www.thepsychologist.org.uk/archive/archive_home.cfm/volumeID_15-editionID_88-ArticleID_477-getfile_getPDF/thepsychologist%5Cnov02Golombok.pdf (accessed 28 May 2014).

Golombok, S. (2003) Children with Lesbian Parents: A Community Study. *Developmental Psychology,* 39(1): 20–33.

Guasp, A. (2010) *Different Families. The Experiences of Children with Lesbian and Gay Parents,* London: Stonewall/Centre for Family Research.

James, A. (2011) Agency. In J. Qvortrup, W.A. Corsaro, and M.-S. Honig (eds), *The Palgrave Handbook of Childhood Studies.* Basingstoke: Palgrave Macmillan.

Kane, E. (2013) *Rethinking Gender and Sexuality in Childhood.* London: Bloomsbury.

Morrow, V. (2009) Children, Young People and their Families in the UK. In H. Montgomery and M. Kellett (eds), *Children and Young People's Worlds: Developing a Framework for Integrated Practice.* Bristol: Policy Press/Open University.

Nieto, S. (1994) Affirmation, Solidarity and Critique: Moving Beyond Tolerance in Multicultural Education. *Multicultural Education,* 1(4): 9–12, 35–38.

Nutbrown, C. and Clough, P. (2013) *Inclusion in the Early Years.* London: Sage.

Pre-school Learning Alliance (2011) *Guide to the Equality Act and Good Practice.* London: Pre-school Learning Alliance.

Prout, A. and James, A. (1997) A New Paradigm for the Sociology of Childhood? Provenance, Promise and Problems. In A. James and A. Prout (eds), *Constructing and Reconstructing Childhood.* Abingdon: Routledge.

Qvortrup, J. (2011) Childhood as Structural Form. In J. Qvortrup, W.A. Corsaro, and M.-S. Honig (eds), *The Palgrave Handbook of Childhood Studies.* Basingstoke: Palgrave Macmillan.

Robinson, K. (2002) Making the Invisible Visible: Gay and Lesbian Issues in Early Childhood Education. *Contemporary Issues in Early Childhood,* 3(3): 414–434.

Rogoff, B. (2003) *The Cultural Nature of Human Development.* Oxford: Oxford University Press.

Short, L. (2007) Lesbian Mothers Living Well in the Context of Heterosexism and Discrimination: Resources, Strategies and Legislative Change. *Feminism and Psychology,* 17(57): 57–74.

Solomon, A. (2013) *Far from the Tree; A Dozen Kinds of Love.* London: Chatto and Windus.

Stonewall (2014) *What is Homophobia?* [Online]. Available at http://www.stonewall.org.uk/at_home/sexual_orientation_faqs/2697.asp (accessed 9 June 2014).

Understanding Prejudice (2014) *The Psychology of Prejudice: An Overview* [Online]. Available at http://www.understandingprejudice.org/apa/english/page24.htm (accessed 8 September 2014).

United Nations (2014) *Convention on the Rights of the Child* [Online]. Available at http://www.ohchr.org/EN/ProfessionalInterest/Pages/CRC.aspx (accessed 25 June 2014).

Wolpert, E. (2005) *Start Seeing Diversity. The Basic Guide to an Anti-Bias Classroom.* St Paul, MN: Redleaf Press.

3 | The legal background[1]

Good equalities practice is not just a desired feature of early years practice, it is also part of the legal obligation that settings have. This legal obligation that rests on settings and guides their practice is a combination of different obligations. There is a legal obligation on behalf of the setting in respect of the rights of the children who use the nursery or pre-school and there is also an obligation in regard of the rights of the employees of the setting and of the families who use the setting.

This multi-faceted role can be daunting to the new owner or manager of a setting and can result in many misunderstandings or interpretation of equalities practice as 'We can't say this' or 'We are not allowed to do that' comments that pass as hearsay from setting to setting.

This chapter aims to clarify some of the issues and clearly explain the main policies and legislation that are associated with LGBT diversity in the early years. We will also look at the history of legislation that has affected gay men and lesbians. In writing this chapter, we have consulted Stonewall and also drawn on the most up-to-date information that we could find. Inevitably new legislation and guidance comes into being during and since this book has been written, and this chapter is no substitute for individuals carrying out their own research. At no point does this chapter offer legal advice; it just presents our own interpretation of legal requirements.

1 We are indebted to Stonewall for providing help and support in the writing of this chapter.

Background to current equalities legislation

There can be a tendency from practitioners to see laws and statutory guidance as an outside view that is imposed on a setting; something to add to an already heavy workload and curtail the direct contact time that is spent with children. In fact, current equality laws are a statement of how society views those whose rights have historically been marginalized or ignored. Legislation in itself cannot change behaviour or an attitude, but what it can do is draw attention to redressing a balance and saying what is acceptable and unacceptable at a current time.

In this way governments draw up current legislation after consultation with a range of organisations and associated bodies with the aim of reflecting public opinion and the idea that the majority of the population will support it. In addition to the legislation, governments can produce further information through books of guidance or codes of practice. These seek to outline examples of the way that the Act can be interpreted and applied to practice by the people that it will affect. These codes of practice are especially helpful to local authorities that are often at the start of the journey of interpreting an Act and thinking on how this will result in changes to their practice. They then filter this information on to their service users – to the managers and leaders of early years settings, for example.

There are also many 'guides to' that talk the layperson through an Act. The Act itself can be written in dense 'legal speak' that is often hard to understand. Sometimes the way that it has been written is not clear and then it can be tested; these are sometimes referred to as 'loopholes' and people use these ambiguities of meaning to bring their own cases and see if an Act can be challenged in its interpretation of facts.

Ultimately a law is only as effective as those who understand it and take steps to ensure that it is adhered to, and equality law will be continually tested with what is called 'case law'. This is the way that laws can be interpreted by individuals or groups, who then seek to test their interpretation by taking a case to court and citing a specific Act. The result of this 'testing' is that the decision made in this case will be a guideline for other similar cases as they arise.

A recent example of this is an ongoing case by two teenagers who are seeking a judicial review against increased university tuition fees, as they argue that this will disadvantage students from poorer homes and that this will impact on students from ethnic minorities who are disproportionally from lower income homes (Shepherd 2011).

There are other examples of the Equality Act 2010 being used to challenge Government cuts in public spending; again, these are based on the argument that cuts will disadvantage an already disadvantaged group.

The Equality Act 2010

This Act brought together other equalities legislation that practitioners will be familiar with, such as the Disability Discrimination Act, and also enhanced and changed some aspects of equalities law. One of the changes was that if someone belonged to more than one of the groups that fell in the 'protected characteristic' category (see below), then they didn't have to use more than one piece of legislation in their argument.

The Equality Act is a mixture of rights and responsibilities that have:

- Stayed the same – for example, direct discrimination still occurs when 'someone is treated less favorably than another person because of a protected characteristic'
- Changed – for example, employees will now be able to complain of harassment even if it is not directed at them, if they can demonstrate that it creates an offensive environment for them
- Been extended – for example, associative discrimination (direct discrimination against someone because they associate with another person who possesses a protected characteristic) will cover age, disability, gender reassignment and sex as well as race, religion and belief and sexual orientation
- Been introduced for the first time – for example, the concept of discrimination arising from disability, which occurs if a disabled person is treated unfavourably because of something arising in consequence of their disability.

(ACAS 2011)

There is an excellent guide to the Equality Act provided by ACAS – the Advisory, Conciliation and Arbitration Service. It has useful guides for employers that are not related to early years but provide a sound platform to establishing good practice.

In this chapter, we will be focusing on the part of the Act that looks at LGBT diversity. Lindon (2012) provides a chapter that gives a clear overall guide to the Equality Act and looks in detail at the way that it could apply to an early years setting in terms of all of the protected characteristics. It is always good to remember that what is relevant to equalities practice must include LGBT diversity and also that 'marriage' when mentioned is also civil partnership.

Two of the protected characteristics that are listed in the Equality Act are specifically related to LGBT diversity.

Activity

On your own or as a staff activity, can you think which protected characteristics these are? It is an also an interesting activity to try and list all nine. The full list is in the Government website (see Equality Act 2010).

Points of reflection

Gender reassignment and sexual orientation are the two characteristics that clearly concern this book, as they relate to LGBT diversity. Did your staff team manage to identify these? Does either of them surprise you? We wonder if you or other staff members think that neither of these issues have anything to do with working with preschool children. We hope that through reading this book you will be able to see that you are helping children with their education and development, not just in the moment and for the period that they are with you, but also for the future, the person that they will be and the world that they will live in, and that is why good inclusive practice is so important.

In terms of the rights of the families who use the setting and the staff who work there the relevance of the Equality Act should be apparent. The following case studies attempt to give a practical application of points of the Act. The most important point to remember is the one that we made at the beginning of the chapter. This Act is not there to frighten you that you are doing something 'wrong' or, if you are a manager or leader of a setting, worry you that members of staff will make cases against you or the nursery. Rather, this important Act is there to acknowledge and protect the rights of those who historically haven't had the protection that other members of the community in the UK take for granted.

Case study 3.1

Ben is a room leader in a daycare setting. He recently married his partner Liam and asked the manager for leave so that they can go on a honeymoon following the wedding. His request is refused, as it is the nursery 'busy time'. Another room leader has their request for leave for the same period granted so that she can go on a hen outing. When Ben queries this, he is told that the other member of staff is more junior than him and that he cannot be spared in the same way.

Points for discussion

This action could be challenged under the Equality Act, as it is direct discrimination. Discuss with a staff team that Ben would have to take action against the setting. This is not criminal law, so although it contravenes the Equality Act it is not illegal.

Case study 3.2

Lisa works in a pre-school. She does not conceal the fact that she is gay when she discusses her life, but does not have a partner, so does not take part in general discussions about partners that happen in the staff room. There have been incidents recently where staff members have made homophobic remarks. They have ranged from discussing children's play ('Both girls wanted to dress up as brides and I told them that there had to be a boy as well as a girl'), talking about Wimbledon ('Some of them are so masculine-looking, no wonder they're that way; no man would want them') and discussing same sex parents who use the setting ('It's the children I feel sorry for').

Lisa is a relatively new member of staff and feels loath to challenge these remarks, especially as they are all said in informal situations. She discussed this with the manager at a supervision meeting and the manager said, 'Oh they don't mean any harm. I think they forget that you're that way, as you're so pretty.'

Points for discussion

Lisa could take action against the nursery, as this is clearly harassment. We hope you can see that in terms of LGBT, staff, members' remarks do not have to be always directed at them. The important point is that these remarks make the setting an uncomfortable and offensive environment for them to work in. The excuse of 'Well, I was only joking' or 'I didn't mean you' is not acceptable in this case.

We want to make it clear that we are not trying to curtail all joking or fun within the staff team during their times of relaxation. We are aware that working in early years can be a stressful job and that these moments of leisure are very important. What we are saying is that they do not have to be connected with making disparaging remarks about a group of people who have historically been targeted for abuse and discrimination. An early years setting is not the place for this kind of talk and it reveals deep-seated attitudes from staff members that need to be challenged, as these will inevitably form part of the work that they do with children, however subconsciously.

Important points to remember

Direct discrimination by association

This is when a person is discriminated against because they are thought to have a protected characteristic that in fact they don't have.

> ## Case study 3.3
>
> Tom works in a reception class and has applied for a vacancy in a year 6 class. The deputy head pulls him to one side and asks him if he is sure that he wants to work with the older children, as 'the boys can be very loud and rough and may not respond to someone like you'. When Tom asks what he means, the deputy says, with a laugh, 'Well, you know, someone who is gay.' Tom says that he is not gay, but gets the response, 'Well, we just think you should stay with the babies, as you are so gentle and sweet with them and all of the mums love you there.'
>
> ### Point for discussion
>
> Tom is not gay but is being discriminated against as though he is.

Direct discrimination by association

This is when a person is treated less favourably because they are linked or associated with a person with a protected characteristic.

> ## Case study 3.4
>
> Lou is a room leader in a nursery and has a friend, Marion, who is a transgender woman. Marion is thinking about working in childcare and Lou invited her into the nursery to have a chat and get a feel of

the environment. While Marion was there the other staff in the room started whispering together, and members of staff from other rooms kept coming into the room on various excuses, but while they were there they stared at Marion, and when they were introduced to her just stood there, and then Lou heard them laughing as they left.

Lou felt embarrassed for Marion and cut her visit short. Since then she is aware of conversations stopping as she walks into the staff room and the manager, previously friendly, is now cool towards her and a recent request to go on SENCO training has been turned down with no reason.

Points for discussion

Lou has a case under the Equality Act as she is being treated less favourably because of her association with a person with a protected characteristic.

Further reflection

In Case study 3.3 the person discriminated against was openly gay. It seems as though the Equality Act can only be used if the person has revealed their protected characteristic to their employers. What does your staff team think of this? Does it matter if a staff member makes homophobic comments if no one who is gay is there to hear them? What about when someone is discriminated against because of association with someone else with a protected characteristic? These would be interesting topics for discussion at a staff meeting, as there are implications for many aspects of inclusion that could be debated from this starting point.

Children and Families Act 2014

This is the other main piece of recent legislation that this chapter will look at. As with the Equality Act, this legislation consolidated other pieces of law so that they were together in one place. The changes that have been made that affect parents in the new Act will also affect same sex parents. For example, the introduction of shared parental leave will apply to same sex parents as well. Now that we have looked at the Equality Act 2010, it should be clear that if a same sex parent was refused these rights, then they could make a case under this Act, as it would be direct discrimination.

The provisions in the Children and Families Act will be relevant to early years settings, through their relationships with the families that use the setting but also as employers. If a practitioner is in a same sex relationship and their partner is pregnant, or they are adopting a child together, then the Act makes provision for them to go to clinic appointments and other meetings with their partner and they can ask to change their work times or places if they need to.

Settings should be aware in their dealings with families that any provisions for parents in the Act, or when they are named in anyother Act, for example the Children Act 2004, also applies to same sex parents.

Human Fertilisation and Embryology Act 2008

The law was changed on 6 April 2009, and the new rules on parenthood for lesbian couples apply only to children conceived on or after that date. They allow both lesbian partners to be treated as parents of a child they conceive together in certain circumstances.

(Gamble 2014)

The full implications, and also limits, that this new Act introduced can be found in the main text (also see Human Fertilisation and Embryology Act 2008). There have been some interesting developments concerning the right of a child to contact their donor that may be of interest to practitioners as further research. For the purposes of this chapter, the main issue for early years workers to note is that both mothers can be registered on a child's birth certificate if they were in a civil partnership/marriage when the child was conceived. Previously, the partner who was not the biological parent had to go through the process of adopting the child in order to be legally recognised.

World Health Organisation

It wasn't until 1992 that the World Health Organisation declassified homosexuality as a mental illness. This is important, as when it was considered a mental illness there was a school of thought that such an 'illness' could be 'cured'. There was also a possibility of a gay person being sectioned/institutionalised for being gay, so declassifying being gay as a mental illness was an important legal milestone (European Parliament 2011).

One kind of 'cure' was through reparative therapy. This therapy has been discredited by all reputable organizations, but is still practised by some far right and extreme religious groups. Stonewall have some interesting and informative material on this now obsolete link between mental illness and being gay (Stonewall 2014a).

There is an important distinction here between reparative therapy that seems to 'cure' gayness and supportive and sensitive counselling that supports an individual, especially a young person, who is exploring their sexuality and thinks that they might be gay.

> Being gay does not, in and of itself, cause mental health problems. Instead, homophobic bullying, rejection from family, harassment at work and poor responses from healthcare professionals are still commonplace for many lesbian, gay and bisexual people.
> (Stonewall 2014b)

It is worth noting that being transgender is still classified as a mental illness by the World Health Organisation. The revised list of mental illnesses is being reconsidered and will be issued in 2015.

Early Years Foundation Stage

We now come to the statutory framework for all settings that care for children from birth to age 5. Throughout the revised EYFS (effective from September 2014), there is an emphasis on enabling individual children to reach their full potential through supporting their learning and development and welfare. We have stated in Chapter 1 how good, inclusive practice benefits all children and that the practice of the setting should be supportive not only to the child that is there at that time, but also the young person and adult that they become. In this way all of the EYFS guidance in the learning and development requirements that relate to equality issues and good inclusive practice includes LGBT diversity, even though it is not specifically mentioned.

Section 3.66 in the previous version of the EYFS made clear statements about the importance of equal opportunities in the section on welfare. In the revised version of the EYFS, this section does not exist and the authors note this with sadness for the lack of emphasis on the importance of promoting good equalities practice as a welfare requirement. It is to be hoped that interested bodies will note this omission and that with consultation future revisions will include this provision.

Ofsted

Ofsted are charged with inspecting registered provision and ensuring that it meets the requirements of the EYFS in terms of learning and development and welfare requirements. This duty has been conferred to it from the Children Act 1989/2004.

On examining the evaluation schedule for inspectors that came into effect in September 2014, there are no specific requirements for settings to acknowledge LGBT diversity or indeed to produce evidence of good equalities practice at all. However, looking at the description of a provision that has been judged 'outstanding', it is clear that much of this practice would be underpinned by proactive and well-thought-out inclusion of the children and families who use the setting.

Outstanding (1)
The provision is better than good because:

- It consistently achieves very high standards across all aspects of its work with exceptional educational programmes for children of all ages. The quality of teaching is consistently of a very high quality, inspirational and worthy of dissemination to other providers.

- Practitioners have very high expectations of themselves and the children. Using their expert knowledge of the areas of learning and a clear understanding of how children learn they provide rich, varied and imaginative experiences for the children.
- Assessment at all ages is precise, sharply focused and includes all those involved in the child's learning. It is monitored and used to secure timely interventions and support, based on a comprehensive knowledge of the child and their family.
- Children are well motivated, very eager to join in and consistently demonstrate the characteristics of effective learning. The extremely sharp focus on helping them to acquire communication and language skills, and on supporting their physical, personal, social and emotional development helps all children make rapid improvement in their learning from their starting points with any gaps closing rapidly. They are exceptionally well prepared for school or the next steps in their learning.

Highly successful strategies engage all parents in their children's learning in the setting and at home.

(Ofsted 2014)

United Nations Convention on the Rights of the Child

In 1989, governments worldwide promised all children the same rights by adopting the UN Convention on the Rights of the Child. These rights are based on what a child needs to survive, grow, participate and fulfil their potential. They apply equally to every child, regardless of who they are, or where they are from.

(UNICEF 2014a)

UNICEF is the only organisation working with children that the Convention recognises, and worldwide all countries except for two have signed up to the Convention.

Activity

Two countries haven't signed. Can you make a guess as to which ones they are?

Answer

Somalia and the USA – discussing this would be an interesting activity at a staff meeting. There is more information on the UNICEF website (2014a), including the dates that countries signed up to the Convention. It is clear that this took some time for some countries.

Looking at the summary of the Convention (UNICEF 2014a), it is clear that many of the 'articles', as they are known, could relate to LGBT diversity. This is an interesting thought, as some of the countries are also listed as places where being gay is illegal.

Activity

Look at the two lists (2014a, 2014b) and the crossover – how do you think the rights of children with families who identify as LGBT are protected in those countries?

Looking at the articles, the relevance to LGBT diversity starts with the second statement:

> Article 2 (Non-discrimination): The Convention applies to all children, whatever their race, religion or abilities; whatever they think or say, whatever type of family they come from. It doesn't matter where children live, what language they speak, what their parents do, whether they are boys or girls, what their culture is, whether they have a disability or whether they are rich or poor. No child should be treated unfairly on any basis.
>
> (UNICEF 2014b)

We think that this could clearly apply to a child where family members identify as LGBT. In fact, articles 4, 5, 8 and 12 clearly can link to LGBT diversity.

Activity

Article 14

Article 14 (Freedom of thought, conscience and religion): Children have the right to think and believe what they want and to practise their religion, as long as they are not stopping other people from enjoying their rights. Parents should help guide their children in these matters. The Convention respects the rights and duties of parents in providing religious and moral guidance to their children. Religious groups around the world have expressed support for the Convention, which indicates that it in no way prevents parents from bringing their children up within a religious tradition. At the same time, the Convention recognizes that as children mature and are able to form their own views, some may question certain religious practices or cultural traditions. The Convention supports children's right to examine their beliefs, but it also states that their right to express their beliefs implies respect for the rights and freedoms of others.

(UNICEF 2014b)

Do you think that LGBT diversity falls into the sphere of 'cultural traditions'?

Discussion

This is an interesting thought and part of the bigger questions that we signpost you to – is being LGBT a moral or cultural decision, or something that a person has no control over and is part of their genetic makeup?

A brief history of legislation in the UK in regard to LGBT diversity

With the recent advent of gay marriage in 2014 and The Equality Act 2010, it is useful to consider how recent this legislation granting the same rights and responsibilities to gay people as heterosexual people is.

The legislative privilege of being heterosexual, and for this not to be an offence, is something many practitioners may not think about. It is reflective to consider that for gay people, gay men especially, this freedom from criminal proceedings just for being openly gay has not always been the case in the UK, and is still not the case in many countries. In 70 of 195 countries in the world, being gay is a crime.

In England and Wales, sexual acts between two adult (aged 21 or over) males with no other people present were made legal in 1967 after the Wolfenden Report. This came into force in Scotland in 1980 and in Northern Ireland in 1982. It wasn't until 2001 that the age of consent for gay men was set at 16 – the same as had been for heterosexual consent since 1885. The Sexual Offences (Amendment) Act 2000 became law in January 2001 in the UK and equalised the age of consent.

The road to equality has not been a steady one of unfolding progression in equality law following 1967. In 1988, Margaret Thatcher's government bought in Section 28 and this made it illegal to 'promote' homosexuality in schools. This chapter is not the place for an in-depth discussion of this ruling, but it is interesting to note that many of the lesbians and gay men who are now working in and leading early years practice suffered as a result of Section 28.

> When I was a teenager in school, I felt that no one was able to support me and that the teachers were too scared to act when I was being bullied. I was treated for depression for a long time in my twenties and I think that it was a direct result of Section 28.
>
> (gay man, manager of a nursery)

Section 28 was finally repealed in 2003, after a long campaign against it. Stonewall was set up in the UK in 1989 to fight against Section 28.

In 2003, the Employment Equality (Sexual Orientation) Act came into force, making it illegal to discriminate against lesbians and gay men in the workplace. This didn't give as much protection to gay people as their heterosexual colleagues, and it wasn't until 2007, with the Equality Act (sexual orientation) Regulations, that parity was achieved.

In 2000, the ban on lesbians and gay men serving in the armed forces was lifted. Until then, lesbians and gay men could not be openly gay, and if their sexuality was revealed they could be dismissed with no recourse to compensation.

Marriage

In 2004, civil partnerships were introduced in the UK, and this was extended to marriage in 2014. The rights that had been introduced with civil partnerships did not extend, but significantly, calling it 'marriage' was a crucial step in equality for gay and lesbian couples. While writing this, there is a new ruling approved where couples with civil partnerships can transfer this to a marriage from December 2014.

Other laws have been passed in very recent years that protect the rights of lesbians and gay men in terms of goods and services and incitement to homophobic hatred.

Conclusion

We hope that reading this chapter will provide material for reflective discussion in staff meetings and also individual consideration of the issues raised. Here are some interesting points to think about as a result of reading this chapter:

- The great disparity that there has been, until very recently, between the rights of the heterosexual community and those of lesbians and gay men. Think about the fact that there are gay men alive who have experienced both the criminalisation of gay relationships and also the legalisation of gay marriage.

- The fact that this disparity of rights still continues in many countries around the world, and that this is not limited to so called 'Third World' countries – 13 states in the USA have anti-sodomy laws on their statute books. Some of these countries have also signed up to protect the rights of the child. Is this possible?

- The legacy of Section 28.

- With the advent of equal marriage rights, staff in a setting can no longer presume that when a parent or a child uses the word 'marriage' that this refers to one between a man and a woman.

- Joking and remarks in the staff room, however good-humoured they are meant, can first contravene the Equalities Act and second reveal that staff have deep-seated prejudices that need to be challenged. The use of language is important, and can form part of a network of humiliation and discrimination for people who identify as LGBT. Think how the word 'gay' is used.

- Linked to this is the fact that, even with these legal rights in primary schools today, Stonewall reports that teachers say that more than two in five children (44%) experience homophobic bullying in schools but that they (the teachers) have never had any training on how to deal with this.

References

ACAS (2011) *The Equality Act 2010* [Online]. Available at http://m.acas.org.uk/index.aspx?articleid=3017 (accessed 7 September 2014).

Equality Act (2010) *Equality Act 2010* [Online] Available at http://www.legislation.gov.uk/ukpga/2010/15/section/4 (accessed 24 June 2014).

European Parliament (2011) *European Parliament: World Health Organization must stop treating transgender people as mentally ill* [Online] Available at http://www.lgbt-ep.eu/press-releases/who-must-stop-treating-transgender-people-as-mentally-ill/ (accessed 11 August 2014).

Gamble, N. (2014) *Donor insemination and IVF Treatment* [Online]. Available at http://www.stonewall.org.uk/at_home/parenting/2626.asp (accessed 25 June 2014).

Human Fertilisation and Embryology Act (2008) [Online]. Available at http://www.legislation.gov.uk/ukpga/2008/22/ (accessed 30 January 2015).

Lindon, J. (2012) *Equality and Inclusion in Early Childhood*. Oxon: Hodder Education.

Ofsted (2014) *Evaluation Schedule for Inspections of Registered Early Years Provision* [Online]. Available at http://www.ofsted.gov.uk/resources/using-early-years-evaluation-schedule-guidance-for-inspectors-of-registered-early-years-settings-req (accessed 25 June 2014).

Shepherd, J. (2011*) Tuition Fees: Teenagers Seek Human Rights Judicial Review* [Online]. http://www.theguardian.com/education/2011/feb/24/tuition-fees-human-rights-university (accessed 24 June 2014).

Stonewall (2014a) *Reparative Therapy* [Online]. Available at http://www.healthylives.stonewall.org.uk/for-patients/your-health/reparative-therapy.aspx (accessed 11 August 2014).

Stonewall (2014b) *Mental Health: Stonewall Health Briefing* [Online]. Available at http://www.healthylives.stonewall.org.uk/includes/documents/cm_docs/2012/m/mental-health.pdf (accessed 11 August 2014).

UNICEF (2014a) *Fact Sheet: A Summary of the Rights under the Convention on the Rights of the Child* [Online]. Available at http://www.unicef.org/crc/files/Rights_overview.pdf (accessed 31 August 2014).

UNICEF (2014b) *UN Convention on the Rights of the Child* [Online]. Available at http://www.unicef.org.uk/UNICEFs-Work/Our-mission/UN-Convention (accessed 31 August 2014).

4 | We are family

When I (Kath) was 17 years old and training to be a nursery nurse, a friend of my mother's got a new job as a lecturer training nursery teachers at a prestigious teacher training college. Previously she had been a senior member of staff at a state-maintained nursery school in a culturally diverse inner-city area. I had done work experience at this school and it was hugely influential in my commitment to my decision to train to work with young children. My mother's friend took an interest in my career and talked to me about her new job. She once told me about an exciting new course they were teaching entitled 'The Family'. Apparently they had had a lively discussion about what exactly was a family and had come up with the definition: 'Whoever is behind the front door'. She gave the example of an old lady living with her much-loved cat. This definition allowed the old lady and her cat to be acknowledged as family.

My parents had separated when I was 14 years old and, at 17, this was still painful for me. I suggested to my mother's friend that not all families live behind the same door and that sometimes family members live apart. Her reply to this was, 'We're not talking about your family, dear.' I was devastated by this, but said nothing further. In her noble attempts to be inclusive and to acknowledge that pets can be a very important part of family life, she had failed to see that her definition of family was in fact very exclusive.

This personal story is relevant here, as it encourages us to think carefully about how we define 'family', who we include in our definition and who we exclude from it. You are asked to think about these issues in relation to families with LGBT parents. While this might be challenging, it is important to think about the impact on children of not having their families recognised and of getting the idea that we are not talking about their families in the many messages we convey about family life.

This chapter considers the many ways families with LGBT parents are formed, focusing on families where the children were born in previous heterosexual relationships, families where the children were born as a result of insemination and families where the children are fostered or adopted. Some examples of good practice are then considered and things to think about are proposed. The issue of what children call their parents is then explored and it is suggested that it is of central importance that practitioners acknowledge the varied ways that children name their parents. Your thinking in this chapter is supported with three case studies.

LGBT parent families

Like all families, LGBT parent families come in many shapes and sizes. Some will have many children, some will have only one. There will be families dealing with all the issues that any other family may be facing. Poverty, ill health and disability, poor housing, parental separation, redundancy, low pay, mental health issues and many others are all issues that LGBT parent families may struggle with. There will also be births, deaths, marriages, birthdays, parties, holidays, moving house, starting a new job or school, and all the other life events that all families experience. As 11-year-old Joe tells us of his life with his two fathers, 'We go to the shops too – we're more the same than different!'

Before moving on to look at who LGBT parent families are, a word about terminology. Much of the writing on LGBT parent families refers to 'LGBT families' or 'lesbian and gay families' or 'lesbian and gay homes and households' (Bos and Sandfort 2010; Brown 2007; Kane 2013; Leddy et al. 2012; Lindon 2012). We have chosen to distance ourselves from this terminology, as it is inaccurate to name these families by the sexuality or gender identity of the parents. In the same way as it would not be appropriate to refer to a family with a disabled parent as a 'disabled family' or a family with a single parent as a 'single family', it is not appropriate to name a family with LGBT parents as an LGBT family. We therefore make clear whose sexuality or gender identity we are referring to, even though this is a little more long-winded! The only exception to this is when we are quoting directly from the work of others.

Children born in previous heterosexual relationships

Many children with LGBT parents were born to heterosexual parents, where one or both parents then came out as lesbian, gay, bisexual or transgender. Sometimes the parents' relationship ends as a result of this and new families, either as single parents or with new partners, are formed (see Case study 4.1). For the children in these situations, many of the issues of parents separating and forming new relation-ships are the same as they are for any children whose parents separate. It is important to recognise that insecurity at this time will largely be due to the separation, possibly involving moving house, new childcare or school and getting used to new relationships. As Chris, now 12, recalls, 'When mum first met Alice, I was only 3 so I was a bit jealous, as I wanted my mum to myself but now I think of her as my stepmum.'

Sonia explains how important she found it to be honest with her children throughout the process of the relationship breakdown:

> They knew me as their dad and it was quite hard to explain that I was now going to be living as a woman. They're great kids, though, and they adapted really well. I told them they could ask me anything and that I would answer as honestly as I could. I think that helped. It also helped that me and their mum stayed good friends. That helped them see that it was OK.

Case study 4.1

Lily is 30 months old and attends a day care setting from 8.30 am to 4.30 pm Monday to Thursday. She is looked after by her maternal grandmother on Fridays. Both her parents work and they separated when Lily was 10 months old. They share care for Lily equally and she stays with them on alternate weeks.

Lily's mother and father, Leon and Cheryl, get on well and have maintained a good relationship throughout their separation. Their main concern is Lily's wellbeing and security. The separation occurred when Leon came out. He is now living with his partner, Kevin. Kevin also has a close bond with Lily. Cheryl lives with her new partner, Phil, and Cheryl is six months pregnant. All four of the significant adults in Lily's life are fully involved in her care and they all fetch her from the nursery regularly.

Recently Lily became upset when Cheryl fetched her from nursery. Lily told her mother that Sue, a new member of staff, asked her who 'that other man' was who had collected her the day before. She had told Sue that he was Daddy's boyfriend. Although Sue hadn't replied in a negative way, Lily was upset that she had been asked who Kevin was, as to her he was just one of her parents.

Cheryl spoke to Lily's keyworker, who explained that Sue had been a bit embarrassed, as she didn't know about the family situation. Cheryl requested that any future questions be addressed to one of them rather than to Lily.

Points to consider

- What could have been done to avoid this situation?
- Why was Sue embarrassed?
- What are *your* feelings about this family?
- How would you ensure that Lily felt accepted and included?

Discussion

Our assumptions about family life can influence our reactions to situations that we deem to be outside the 'norm'. For Lily, her family is the way it is. However, this can make some people feel uncomfortable. Being able to challenge and reflect on your own feelings and attitudes is a crucial part of providing inclusive practice.

Making sure that new staff are aware of who the important adults in a child's life are can help to avoid a situation such as this. It would also be important to talk to Sue about what happened and ask why she was embarrassed by this situation. She may not have knowingly met a family with same sex parents before, or she may have some more deep-seated feelings based on a religious or other belief. It is important that she understands the commitment she has made to inclusive practice by taking on her new role in the setting.

Ways forward

- It could be helpful for Lily's keyworker and Sue to discuss the situation and talk through their thoughts and feelings.

- Circle time could be used to ensure that Lily feels her family is recognised and valued within the setting.

- Resources could be checked to ensure that Lily is able to recognise her family in some of the toys and equipment within the setting.

- Training could be made available for the staff team to support their inclusion of Lily and her family. (See Chapter 6 for more on training.)

Children born as a result of insemination

Increasingly, children are born to LGBT parents through insemination by known or anonymous donor (see Case study 4.2) or through surrogacy. When the donor is known, they may or may not be involved in the child's life. When clinics are used to aid conception, the child is able to receive details of the donor when they become 18 years old. Recent legislation (see Chapter 3) allows both names in a same sex partnership to be on a child's birth certificate. Unlike children whose parents come out after the children are born, children who are conceived through insemination or surrogacy have LGBT parents from the start and the parents are encountering the medical profession and early years practitioners from the beginning. One mother remembers that, when she was pregnant, the doctor questioned her dates and said she must be wrong, that she was a month more pregnant than she thought: 'He got quite angry and asked how I could be so sure. I had only inseminated once, so I really was very sure. I didn't want to tell him that, though.'

For very young children the family they have is seen as the norm. 'Until I went to nursery, I didn't realise my family was unusual. It is only when someone tells you that you are different that you realise it,' says one young person. She remembers that as she got older she was aware that her family wasn't the same as most of the children she knew, and she felt aware of homophobia even though she wouldn't have been able to name it.

Case study 4.2

Gemma and Kumi have been together for nine years. They have two children, who attend the same early years setting for two days a week. Aisha is 36 months and Sam is six months. Gemma is Aisha's biological mother and Kumi is Sam's biological mother. Both children were conceived using the same anonymous donor. Aisha calls Gemma 'Mummy' and Kumi 'Mama'. They will encourage Sam to do the same. Gemma and Kumi share responsibility for the girls equally, although Kumi was on maternity leave until recently and during this time her bond with Aisha grew deeper.

Gemma and Kumi spent a lot of time choosing a nursery for Aisha and it was very important to them that the staff and the ethos were positive about their family. They live in a small town and have encountered some homophobia in the wider community. This got worse when Gemma become pregnant and their neighbours were openly hostile to them. They still cope with this and, recently, when they complained about loud music, the neighbour shouted at them that they should move and let a 'proper family' have their house. Aisha overheard this and has been asking why they aren't a proper family. Gemma and Kumi have informed the nursery about this and have found the setting to be very supportive.

Points to consider

- What role can an early years setting play in supporting families experiencing homophobia?

- What impact could it have on the family's life to be dealing with this homophobia?

- Why is it important to know the way in which children refer to the important adults in their lives?

Discussion

It is important that early years settings acknowledge that homophobia exists, as do many other forms of oppression and prejudice. Even when the setting is positive, it is important to recognise that children might be dealing with very challenging and difficult situations outside the setting and to be aware that this can have a detrimental impact on the child's wellbeing. It will have an impact on Aisha's sense of self to hear that there are people who don't see their family as equal to other families. In addition to this, the stress it places on Gemma and Kumi will impact on the children.

The setting can play a vital role in supporting Aisha and Sam. Making sure the family structure is acknowledged in all aspects of the setting can help counteract the homophobia they experience. Acknowledging family names can be an important aspect of this. Ensuring that Gemma and Kumi are referred to as 'Mummy' and 'Mama' can help the children to feel that their parents are recognised and valued. Mother's day cards, for example, could be an ideal opportunity to do this, with both children making cards for both of their mothers and not just for their biological mother.

Ways forward

- Gemma and Kumi are very proactive in their relationship with the setting. Not all families will be so engaged. It can be useful to think about practice in relation to *all* families and how they can be recognised and supported.

- Will Aisha and Sam see representations of their family in the setting? Photographs, illustrations and other images should reflect all families.

- Do all staff recognise and accept same sex parents? What might need to happen to support this?

Fostering and adoption

Many children with LGBT parents are fostered or adopted. It has never actively been against the law for lesbians and gay men to adopt children; however, it wasn't until the Adoption and Children Act 2005 that unmarried couples (including same sex couples) were allowed to adopt children for the first time (Stonewall, 2014). Before this, unmarried couples and same sex couples could only adopt as single adopters, with only one name on the adoption certificate. Since the Adoption and Children Act 2005, there has been a steady increase in the numbers of LGBT people coming forward as adopters. (See Chapter 3 for further information about legislation.) The Department for Education states that the number of same sex couples adopting has risen from 3 per cent in 2009 to 6 per cent in 2013 (Pink News 2014). In some areas, there has been a proactive effort to encourage the LGBT community to consider fostering and adoption. For example, the West Sussex County Council 'No Barriers' campaign states that 'Foster carers and adoptive parents can come from all walks of life and people from a variety of backgrounds can apply, regardless of their ethnicity, marital status or sexuality' (West Sussex County Council 2014).

Adopting or fostering as LGBT parents is not always an easy path. Some will argue that having LGBT parents is an added burden for children who have already had to deal with difficult and painful situations. It can be challenging to deal with these views while also supporting the child or children newly placed with you. As Clare explains, 'It was really hard work at first. Karly had been through so many changes in her short life, she didn't really trust us to be her permanent parents. This wasn't helped by other people thinking she shouldn't have been placed with us.' Karly, now 14, adds that it took her a long time to trust her mums but that she hated it if people said anything negative about them. If there is an added burden, it is homophobia, not having LGBT parents.

Case study 4.3

Fin and Leroy had been together for 14 years when they first started thinking about adoption. Three years later, they finally had their son placed with them. Michael was 2 years and 10 months when he moved in with them after a short time of getting to know each other. Michael had been in foster care since he was 15 months old, after attempts to keep him with his birth family broke down. Michael was born heroin-dependent and has some developmental delay. He is of dual heritage origin: his birth mother is white British and his birth father is Black British. Fin and Leroy are of similar origin and will be able to support Michael in learning about his ethnic background. He will grow up with his cultural background reflected in his immediate and wider family.

Fin works full-time and Leroy has returned to work part-time after taking adoption leave. Michael attends an early years setting two days a week. This will gradually increase as Michael continues to settle into his new family.

The setting has worked with adoptive families before, but not with an adopting gay couple, and there have been some issues with other parents, although all the staff have been supportive and welcoming.

Points to consider

- What could the setting do to encourage understanding among all the parents using the setting?

- In what ways might this family need support with the intersection of sexuality, race and additional needs? (See Chapter 2 for an explanation of intersectionality and multiple identities.)

- What are your responses to this case study?

Discussion

Fin and Leroy are new to parenting and will need support in the same way any new parents will. They have a child with some developmental delay and this is likely to be of greater concern to them than the fact that they are two men raising a child. Discussion and openness within the staff team and with other parents will be important in supporting this family.

The issues with other parents need to be explored and open communication will be needed in order to encourage Fin and Leroy to feel a valued and welcome part of the setting community.

Ways forward

- Look at your policy in relation to parent partnerships, and consider if anything needs changing.

- Make sure the staff team all understand the issues and provide reading material to support this. (See Chapter 7 for ideas.)

- Check your resources and ensure that Michael will see his family reflected in the setting.

The extended family and the wider community

As well as these situations, it is important to recognise that children in families with heterosexual parents may well have other significant relationships with LGBT people in their wider families and within their communities. As one practitioner explains:

We've got one little girl, Sammy, at our setting who is fetched every Friday by her auntie. Her auntie lives with her female partner and Sammy talks about her aunties a lot, especially now, as they are planning their wedding and Sammy is going to be a bridesmaid, which she is very excited about! We feel it is important that she can share what's important to her in the same way all the children can.

Although it may seem that the majority of children conceived by insemination are young and that older children and adults with LGBT parents were conceived in previous heterosexual relationships, this is by no means the case. While changes in law and technology may be making it easier for LGBT people to become parents, it is not new. A recent newspaper article highlighting the increase in the numbers of lesbian and gay people becoming parents (Brockes 2012) led Shoshana Davidson to start a blog about her experiences growing up with her lesbian mothers.

What is too often missed, is that there are literally hundreds of us who have grown up in LGBT+ families and lived to tell the tale. I'm in my mid-twenties, and I am not even close to being in the first generation of children of LGBT+ parents.

(Davidson 2014)

For practitioners in early years settings, this is worth bearing in mind. A heterosexual parent bringing a child into your setting may have grown up with LGBT parents themselves. The child may spend considerable time with their LGBT grandparents and this may be a significant part of their lives.

Even if children are growing up not knowingly knowing any LGBT people themselves, they will be part of a community and of society generally, and spending their early years in a setting that values diversity, is positive about difference and challenges discrimination of all kinds will have an impact on all children and their families.

While there are many different ways in which LGBT people come to be parents, or other significant people in children's lives, there are some issues that are shared by them and their children. They all live in a society in which homophobia still plays a part and this has to be dealt with in all aspects of life. It is also important to remember that, even though there are many issues particular to families with LGBT parents, there are also many issues that are shared with all parents. LGBT parents will worry about the same things as any parent – am I a good parent, what is a reasonable bedtime, when should I potty-train, how should we deal with tantrums, should our baby sleep in bed with us, when should I wean him, etc.? As one mother explains:

> How well you support your child, whether you listen to them and give them your attention, spend time with them, play with them, read to them and help them to understand their world is what matters. All of that can happen, or not, in any family.

Thinking about your practice

Some LGBT parents will be open about their family and others will be less so. The more inclusive and welcoming a setting, the more likely it is that families will feel safe and comfortable enough to be open. This openness is crucial to the wellbeing of all children.

Respectful educators will include all children; not just children who are easy to work with, obliging, endearing, clean, pretty, articulate, capable, but every child – respecting them for who they are, respecting their language, their culture, their history, *their family*, their abilities, their needs, their name, their ways and their very essence.

(Nutbrown 1996: 54, emphasis added)

What Nutbrown is saying here is that it feels easier to include some children than others. However, if we have a commitment to inclusive practice, sometimes this might involve challenging ourselves and thinking about who we find easy to include and who we find harder to include. Among the staff of an early years setting or within a group of early childhood studies students, there will be a variety of opinions about families with LGBT parents, about children who have one or two gay or lesbian parents, about people who may be very open about their sexuality or gender identity, about the impact this may have on other parents and children, and even about their feelings about their own sexuality.

- Spend some time thinking about your reactions to these issues.
- What would your feelings be if you were working with a family with LGBT parents?
- Why would you have these feelings?
- What might you need to think about in order to support your inclusive practice with all children and families?

We might like to imagine we are all open and inclusive and that we would not let any negative feelings we do have affect our work. What do you think about the following statements from practitioners when a child with two mothers joined their early years setting?

1. I don't really agree with it myself, but I'd never let that show in my work. It's not the child's fault, is it?

2. Well, I'm a lesbian myself, so I'm really happy when we have gay people using our setting.

3. It's just plain wrong. I don't want any families like that in my setting.

4. We need to work towards being inclusive towards everybody. No child should feel discriminated against because of who they, or their family, are.

5. I think it is fine as long as they aren't too pushy about it.

6. I just feel sorry for the child really. It's not normal, is it?

7. All children need is to feel loved. It really doesn't matter who it is that loves them.

Brown (2007) suggests that people can feel uncomfortable looking at these issues because sexualities other than heterosexuality remain unacceptable in many cultures and religions. It is important to provide time to discuss such issues while at the same time remembering the statutory obligations that all settings have to provide an inclusive environment where no individual or group of individuals is discriminated against. While statement 3 is overtly discriminatory, it is worth considering the more subtle but still discriminatory views expressed in statements 1, 5 and 6. Statement 2 could be seen to imply that it is the job of the LGBT community to address these issues rather than being an issue that is relevant to us all. While statement 7 is positive, it does render LGBT families invisible. Statement 4 shows a commitment to tackling discrimination and working towards inclusion for all children and families.

It is worth remembering that, for the children of LGBT parents, it is 'the prejudices of others that cause them far more distress than their own personal or family characteristics' (Guasp 2010). As one young person explained:

I grew up with two mums and two dads. One of my mums gave birth to me and one of my dads was the donor, but they were all my parents. Until I went to nursery, I was almost entirely surrounded by lesbians, gay men and their kids. We were like one big family. I was very happy and felt loved by lots of people. There were some difficulties, though, but not from my family – it was from other people's attitudes. Although I am straight, I also suffered because of homophobia.

What's in a name?

Young children like to tell the stories of their families. The people important to them are central to these stories. Whether this is to talk about an outing, visiting relatives, a birthday party or a holiday, children need the language to describe these narratives. When working with young children and their families, it is central to recognise the variation and diversity among families and to enable children to talk freely about their lives. Although there are children who can talk about 'Mummy', 'Daddy', 'Granddad' and 'Grandma', there are many others for whom this is not their reality. While many children with heterosexual parents will be outside this norm (single parent families for example), children with LGBT parents may particularly struggle to find a narrative that adequately describes their family.

From birth, children are surrounded by images and messages that suggest that two heterosexual parents are the norm, and that if their family doesn't conform to this they are outside that norm. Gabb (2005) argues that not being able to easily and adequately provide a narrative for their family can be very difficult for children who have a family structure outside the norm. Her research shows young children missing their 'other' mother out of descriptions and drawings of their families in an attempt to convey an image close to that perceived as 'family'. She gives an example of a child drawing himself with his birth mother and his granddad when asked to draw his family. Not only is his other mother invisible in this drawing, but so too is his relationship with her. Gabb suggests that this is, in part, due to a lack of language to describe these family relationships that are outside the familial language we have available. As one young person explains, 'If my mum met a man, I could say I had a new stepdad, but when your mum meets a woman, people don't know what you mean when you say you have a new stepmum. They assume your dad has met someone. If I say she is my mum's friend, that doesn't explain who she is to me!'

However, children can be very creative in developing the language needed to describe the people significant to them, and it is crucial that these names are recognised and valued by early years practitioners. Children born to LGBT parents might have the names they call their parents determined by the parents e.g. 'mummy' and 'mama' (see Case study 4.2). Children whose parents form LGBT relationships after their birth may use names, e.g. 'Daddy' and 'Kevin' (see Case study 4.1) or creative, made-up names as 5-year-old Bill explains, 'I call mummy

"Mummy" and I call Lucy "Mooshy" because it sounds a bit like "Mummy" and a bit like "Lucy"!'

It is important to remember that it may not be an issue to the children or their parents what names are used, as one mum explains:

> The floodgates opened; what I had expected to be a slow trickle was an almighty tidal wave of love. That little person, with his scrunched up face, was mine. Ours. Mine. I was his parent and in that first second that I held him, I knew that all my anxiety over what to be called (Mum? My name? Mama?) was pointless and just didn't matter anymore.
>
> (Stonewall n.d.: 27)

By working closely with children and their parents, the names that children use can be acknowledged by practitioners. This will help to support children in seeing their family as valued equally with any other.

The poem 'Dziecko Child' (Jastrzębska 2004) gives the adult perspective on not having a name that fits easily with who the parent is in the life of the child. The author explains that not having an easily recognisable label for her relationship with her daughter was difficult, and 'it certainly had an impact on me and my sense of entitlement to talk about her as my daughter' (Jastrzębska 2014). Her daughter adds that when she was young she didn't have the language to articulate who the author was in her family. She explains that 'It was difficult to talk about my family because I just didn't have the vocabulary to do so without having to explain absolutely everything, and it just got boring to explain it to people after a while' (Morris 2014).

Dziecko Child
One foot sticking out
from under the jungle pattern duvet,
the rest of you curled
almost foetal in sleep.

There never seems enough time
to notice you. I'm always

hurrying you along, *pick up
your clothes / put your violin away /
time to get up / get ready / go out.*

Secretly, I sometimes think
we look alike, even though
it's not possible and it really
shouldn't matter. Besides,

at your age my hair was
cropped and an array of guns
hung on the wall above my bed.
I wouldn't have been seen dead
with Barbie and Ken, your favourites.

Most nights I speak to *my* mother
on the phone. My friends say that's too much.
*Where I come from, families
are close,* I reply glibly,

too tired to argue with either side.
There are no words for who I am
in your life
and my mother says

you can never be part
of our family. I shampoo
and rinse your hair,
comb out the tangles, despite your tears

and when I pick you up from school
you run into my arms
in your yellow puffa jacket
brighter than daffodils.

(Jastrzębska 2004: 50)

Implications for practice

- It is part of the practitioner's role to be open and welcoming to all families.

- It is central to a child's sense of wellbeing that their family is recognised and valued within their early years setting.

- Resources need to reflect a diverse range of families.

- Children need to know that the names they use for their parents are accepted within the setting.

- A culture of openness needs to be created in a setting so practitioners can safely explore their feelings about these issues.

- Discrimination against LGBT parents and their children needs to be tackled by the setting.

- Even when there are no families with LGBT parents in a setting, it is good equalities practice to reflect on these issues.

Conclusion

This chapter has asked you to consider the diverse number of ways in which LGBT people may become parents, and has asked that you reflect on your role in supporting all families. It has been suggested that an open and reflective ethos needs to be developed in order to allow staff and parents to feel safe and to explore feelings and reactions.

You have been encouraged to think about your practice in terms of acknowledging that good equalities practice for the LGBT community is good equalities practice for all. For children with LGBT parents, having their families and the language they use to describe and name them acknowledged is of central importance.

Thinking about your resources, and whether or not they reflect all families, will help you to assess your setting's approach to equality and diversity. Following chapters will help you to consider these issues in further depth and will encourage you to consider aspects of resources and good practice.

References

Bos, H. and Sandfort, T. (2010) Children's Gender Identity in Lesbian and Heterosexual Two-Parent Families. *Sex Roles,* 62(1–2): 114–126.

Brockes, E. (2012) *Gay Parenting: It's Complicated* [Online]. Available at http://www.theguardian.com/lifeandstyle/2012/apr/20/gay-parenting-emma-brockes (accessed 15 July 2014).

Brown, B. (2007) *Unlearning Discrimination in the Early Years.* Staffordshire: Trentham Books.

Davidson, S. (2014) About this Blog. *My Motherful Family* [Blog]. Available at http://mymotherfullfamily.wordpress.com/about/ (accessed 15 July 2014).

Gabb, J. (2005) Lesbian M/Otherhood: Strategies of Familial-Linguistic Management in Lesbian Parent Families. *Sociology,* 39(4): 585–603.

Guasp, A. (2010) *Different Families. The Experiences of Children with Lesbian and Gay Parents.* London: Stonewall/Centre for Family Research.

Jastrzębska, M. (2004) *Syrena.* Bradford: Redbeck Press.

Jastrzębska, M. (2014) Email to Kath Tayler. 18 June 2014.

Kane, E. (2013) *Rethinking Gender and Sexuality in Childhood.* London: Bloomsbury.

Leddy, A., Gartrell, N. and Bos, H. (2012) Growing up in a Lesbian Family: The Life Experiences of the Adult Daughters and Sons of Lesbian Mothers. *Journal of LGBT Family Studies,* 8: 243–257.

Lindon, J. (2012) *Equality and Inclusion in Early Childhood.* Oxon: Hodder Education.

Morris, E. (2014) Email to Kath Tayler. 3 July 2014.

Nutbrown, C. (1996) *Respectful Educators – Capable Learners: Children's Rights and Early Education.* London: Sage.

Pink News (2014) *England: Number of Gay Couples Adopting Children Doubles* [Online]. Available at http://www.pinknews.co.uk/2014/03/03/england-number-gay-couples-adopting-children-doubles/ (accessed 27 April 2014).

Stonewall (n.d.) *Pregnant Pause: A Guide for Lesbians on how to get Pregnant.* London: Stonewall.

Stonewall (2014) *Adoption and Fostering* [Online]. Available at http://www.stonewall.org.uk/at_home/parenting/2624.asp (accessed 27 April 2014).

West Sussex County Council (2014) *There are no Barriers to Changing a Child's Life* [Online]. Available at http://www.westsussex.gov.uk/your_council/news_and_events/news/2014_archive/february_2014/there_are_no_barriers_to_chang.aspx (accessed 19 May 2014).

5 | Thinking about practice with children and families

All early years practitioners will be familiar with the ideal of providing inclusive settings and of engaging in inclusive practice. All will have ideas about what this means and how we go about it. In its narrowest form, inclusive practice relates to working to include children with special educational needs into mainstream settings. In its broadest sense it relates to thinking about how we work with all aspects of diversity and difference, how we challenge our own preconceptions, how we reflect and think critically, and how we respectfully engage with all children, all parents, all practitioners, all settings and the communities we are part of. Nutbrown and Clough suggest that inclusion may be seen as 'the *unified drive* towards maximal participation in and minimal exclusion from early years settings, from school and society' (2013: 8, emphasis in original). This broad and general definition allows us to think reflectively about who might easily be included and who might be excluded from our settings.

Activity

Think about who might be included or excluded from your setting. Discuss this with your team. Some categories might be more contentious than others; some might be included in some contexts and excluded in others. Compile a list of people who may be excluded and discuss any of these complexities as they arise.

Discussion

Nutbrown and Clough (2013) provide the following list, while clarifying that it is not exhaustive and making it clear that there are many other areas that could be added.

- achievement
- age
- challenging behaviour
- disability
- disaffection
- emotional and behavioural difficulty
- employment
- gender
- housing
- language
- mental health
- obesity
- physical impairment
- poverty
- race/ethnicity
- religion
- sexual orientation
- social class
- Special Educational Need.

(Nutbrown and Clough 2013: 9)

How does this compare to the list you came up with? Did you identify any areas that you think are particularly well included in your setting? What about those that may be excluded? Did you have any disagreements about any of the groups you identified? What complexities did you identify? You may have felt that in some settings a particular group is excluded, while they are not in another setting. For example, a single sex nursery class attached to a private girls' school will exclude boys and all those who cannot afford to pay for private education, a religious setting may exclude those whose families don't follow that religion, or a setting in an old building with many stairs may exclude a child with physical disabilities.

Inclusive practice

The crucial thing to consider when thinking about your inclusive practice is that it can never be something that is 'done'; it requires ongoing commitment and reflection.

> Inclusion is always in a 'state of becoming'. There can be no such thing as a fully inclusive, 'arrived-at' institution or society. In early education and care, practitioners, families and children are constantly working in a state of 'becoming inclusive' for new challenges and new exclusionary factors can confront settings at any point.
>
> (Nutbrown and Clough 2013: 3)

Thinking about inclusive practice in relation to LGBT issues can be an area that is, for many practitioners, a new challenge and one that may not have been thought about in terms of early years education and care.

The Early Years Foundation Stage (EYFS) states that

> Providers must have and implement a policy, and procedures, to promote equality of opportunity for children in their care . . . The policy should cover: how the individual needs of all children will

be met . . .; arrangements for reviewing, monitoring and evaluating the effectiveness of inclusive practices that promote and value diversity and difference; how inappropriate attitudes and practices will be challenged; and how the provision will encourage children to value and respect others.

(DfE 2012: 26)

The newly revised EYFS came into force in September 2014, and in this version the section on equal opportunities has been removed. This includes the above section on challenging inappropriate attitudes and encouraging children to respect and value others. However, the introduction does state that providers must provide 'equality of opportunity and anti-discriminatory practice, ensuring that every child is included and supported' (cited in Meleady 2014: 14). Meleady goes on to remind us that, despite these changes to the EYFS, all settings have a legal obligation to follow 'the Equality Act 2010, the Education and Inspection Act 2006, the UN Convention of the Rights of the Child 1989, and the Human Rights Act 1998' (2014: 14). (See Chapter 3 for more information on legislation.)

Good practice with children and their families

Chapter 6 will consider good practice in terms of leadership and good practice with colleagues. As good practice in any area of early years education and care starts with the child, we want you to consider these issues first and read the next chapter, which covers working with colleagues, while keeping the issues you explore here firmly in mind. In this chapter we consider how good inclusive practice around LGBT equality is of benefit to the children in your setting; not just children with LGBT parents, but *all* children. As Nutbrown and Clough tell us, 'Difference is of interest to children, and the recognition of difference as positive rather than negative is an important aim for early childhood professionals' (2013: 13). It is important to acknowledge that children notice difference and not to see this as a problem. It is the values we place on difference that can create problems, not the differences in themselves. If we define the problem as being about children noticing difference, we deny ourselves the opportunity to ask questions and think through what options we have in terms of response (Wolpert 2005).

Lindon (2012) suggests that a crucial aspect of working toward inclusive practice is reflective practice. The reflective practitioner, she argues, is someone who is willing to think about the different ways an issue could be approached and is able to discuss these options in their team or network.

Activity

Read through the following brief scenarios. Think about them in relation to the potential impact on the children in the settings. Clearly situations such as these will have an impact on parents and practitioners as well, but here the focus is the children. What messages do you think these situations convey to the children? What do they say about who is valued?

* The staff know I'm gay but we never talk about it. The children don't know. In my last nursery one family withdrew their child because they found out I was gay. I wasn't allowed to change nappies. I didn't feel supported or that they were on my side.
  (gay male early years practitioner).

* We felt like they made assumptions. I was the 'real' mummy and Heather was the 'other mummy'. That's not how we introduced ourselves, but that's how they treated us. That upset us and our boys.
  (parents of two boys at an early years setting).

* I overheard some parents saying that Gregg and Stephen shouldn't have been allowed to adopt and that it wasn't fair on the child. I wanted to challenge them but I didn't know what to say.
  (early years practitioner)

- In the staffroom we get a lot of the joking kind of thing where some people say, 'Oh, little Jonny was in the tutu again today – he's going to turn out gay.' I hate it and sometimes I say something, but they just say they're only joking and I take it too seriously.
(early years practitioner)

- The lesbian parents of one of my key children got married recently. I wanted to put photos up like we do when other families have celebrations, but my manager said it was too challenging for some of our families.
(early years practitioner)

- When we were looking for a nursery for our little girl, one of the nurseries told us it would be better if we didn't tell other parents about our 'situation'. We couldn't believe it! Obviously, we went elsewhere!
(lesbian mother)

Discussion

When you first looked at these scenarios, you may have felt that they don't really have an impact on the children and that the situations as they are described take place between adults and do not concern the children. However, by reflecting at a deeper level you may have thought about the way in which the ethos of the setting in which situations such as these can arise will be conveying something about equality and diversity to the children. Consider the ethos of a setting where a practitioner is not allowed to change a baby's nappy when it needs changing or where a child's play preferences are a matter for staffroom banter. What messages is a child receiving when not all parents are valued equally, where some celebrations are perceived of higher importance than others? What happens when discriminatory values of the adults in the setting are left unchallenged?

From the perspective of the child whose mothers looked elsewhere when they received a discriminatory response from a setting, she may be unaware of this situation and clearly her parents are committed to finding a setting that will value their family. However, for the children that are currently in the setting, they are spending their early childhood in an environment that doesn't value full diversity and doesn't share a commitment to challenging discrimination. This is why we argue here that these issues are relevant to all children and all families, and not simply to those where the parents have openly identified as LGBT.

What might good practice look like?

Case study 5.1

Phoenix Nursery is a 20-place setting in central Brighton. It originally catered for the children of students and staff at Brighton University, but in the last two years has opened up to the local community. They have a small staff team, one of whom has Early Years Teacher Status, one has a BA in Early Years and the manager has a Foundation Degree in Early Years. They have one large, bright room, a smaller room, family area, kitchen and bathroom, and a large, enclosed garden with a variety of different areas.

Their *Nursery Handbook* states that they aim to 'provide an anti-bias learning environment, which is safe, stimulating and monitored to meet the needs of all' (University of Brighton 2013: 4).Their Inclusion and Diversity Policy in the handbook says that the nursery staff:

recognise the important role they play in promoting the understanding of, and having a commitment to, the principles of equality and freedom from discrimination on the grounds of nationality, religion, culture, race, gender, sexuality, physical ability, marital and parental status, health, social class, language or race. We are committed to providing a loving and positive learning environment, free from prejudice, discrimination and fear, in which all children, their families and the staff feel accepted, respected and valued.

(2013: 24)

Amongst other ways, they aim to do this by:

- Acting as positive role models ourselves. Monitoring our actions and language in regard to working with all the children, parents/carers, visitors, other professionals and each other.

- Responding to (and challenging) discriminatory behaviour or remarks appropriately . . .

- Carefully selecting resources that give the children and others a balanced view of the world . . .

- Providing materials that help children to develop their self-respect and to respect others, and by avoiding stereotypes and derogatory picture messages or words about any individual or group.

- Recognise that many different types of families successfully love and care for their children.

(2013: 24)

The nursery has a named equalities representative, who has taken part in local authority equalities training. The nursery follows all Equal Opportunities guidance provided by the University and all relevant equalities legislation.

Their positive and proactive approach has helped to create a friendly and welcoming atmosphere where all feel welcomed. They currently have two families with same sex parents and have previously had an adopted child with same sex parents. They suggest that an open approach to this has supported their practice.

They see the following as crucial to a successful approach to equality:

- good communication and listening to all sides of a story

- everyone should have a voice; everyone has their own view

- using appropriate and accurate language

- good parent partnerships and parental involvement

- good settling-in process where you get to know families and acknowledge names children use for their parents, e.g. mum and mummy; respect how parents introduce themselves

- information on the setting's website

- the staff team need to develop reflective practice; ask yourself if there are ways to improve practice

- using a reflective book where staff can write things that have happened

- regular staff meetings

- staff going on training and conferences

- displays to include all families within the setting, e.g. one family with two mothers went to London for a celebration; photographs of this were put on the board

- use posters and other resources that reflect diversity.

Points to consider

- What does your equalities policy look like? Does it include all families and staff?

- Do you have good communication in your team?

- Do you feel able to discuss these issues in an open and honest way?

- Does everyone have a voice?

- Do you and your team view yourselves as positive role models?

- Do you feel comfortable challenging discriminatory remarks from children, parents or other staff?

- Do your resources reflect diversity? Will all children recognise themselves and their families in your resources?

- Do you have respectful parent partnerships?

- Do you have an ethos of reflecting on and continually updating your practice?

- What do your displays convey about your approach to equality?

Discussion

Having a clear equalities policy is a good start, but unless it is acted upon, it is meaningless. All members of staff need to be committed to the ethos of the setting and clear opportunities for open and honest discussion are part of this. Everyone needs to feel comfortable and confident that their views will be listened to and that any challenging will be done sensitively and appropriately. Resources need to be regularly checked for bias or for discriminatory language and images.

Case study 5.1 is based on an interview with two members of staff from Phoenix Nursery in Brighton. They suggest several ways in which they believe their approach to equality and diversity works. As you read these ideas, you may find it useful to think about how they relate to your own practice with families and children. Are there things you already do? Are there areas you can improve on? How could you approach any changes that you feel need making?

Communication

Communication is central to any team that works well together. How you communicate with families and children will set the tone and ethos of your setting. Lindon suggests that 'Effective equality practice will partly be led by how you set a good example in positive communication and deal with words or actions that could undermine children's sense of self-worth' (2012: 116). Children notice and are interested in difference and will openly comment on these perceived differences. Your responsibility as a practitioner is to answer in a clear and simple way without embarrassment or discomfort.

In thinking about communication, you need to think about your responses to, for example, a child saying to another child, 'A boy can't marry another boy.'

- Keep your responses clear and simple, e.g. 'Yes, a man can marry another man if that's what both of them want.' Then ask if they have understood or want to ask any more questions.

- Make sure your responses are accurate. In the UK, same sex marriage is now legal. In other parts of the world, this isn't the case.

- Think about your own feelings and make sure any complexity to how you feel about the issue doesn't influence your response to the children.

- Avoid responding with ways which undermine the child or make them feel bad about what they have said, e.g. don't say something like, 'If Sam wants to marry Sean, that's fine. Don't be mean to him.'

- Model supportive and empathetic responses. The more children are spoken to with kindness, the more they will speak to others in the same way.

Parent partnerships

Relationships with all families are crucial to the way in which a commitment to equality and diversity will operate. This links closely with communication. From the point at which a parent enquires about your setting, you will be communicating with them, and through this you will be conveying the ethos of your setting. By being clear about your openness to all families, you will be saying that all families are welcome and that no family will be discriminated against or excluded. Not all parents will be able to be an active part of the life of a setting, so it is crucial that important information like your equality policy is available on the setting website or in leaflets. A good parent partnership will have multiple ways of building that partnership and not be dependent on parents being able to regularly come into the setting.

The likelihood is that you will be working with families with one parent, families where English is not the home language, families where someone has a disability or illness, families who are travellers, families from a range of cultures and faiths, and many other situations. By setting your work with families with LGBT parents into this wider context, you are showing your openness and willingness to work with *all* families who use your setting and who live in the community of which you are a part.

Developing good parent partnerships takes time and is a process that continues for the whole time the family is using the setting. Often the partnership will start with the setting's settling-in process. This may include home visits, which is an ideal opportunity to get to know who is important in the child's life. Some settings also use family photographs as part of a display, showing that 'all families are welcome here'. As Shana says, 'It was nice to know our photo would be up with all the others, so that there was no misunderstanding about the fact that our son had two mums.' However, it is always important to check that families are happy for their photograph to be displayed, as not all people want to be 'out'.

As discussed in detail in Chapter 4, it is very important to acknowledge the names that children with LGBT parents use to refer to their parents. The settling-in process is an ideal time to make sure you have got this right, and that all staff know and understand the importance of this. The child's key person will be a link between the child, the family and the setting, and it is crucial that this is a positive relationship based on mutual respect.

Reflective practice

As described above, good inclusive practice is highly dependent on good communication with children and families and effective parent partnerships. The extent to which this happens will depend greatly on practitioners' ability to reflect on and think about practice (see Case study 5.2). The issues addressed in this book can be challenging, and it is important to start by acknowledging that and, by recognising that, you don't always feel confident in handling some of the situations that arise.

- You may feel very comfortable recognising that children with LGBT parents are part of your setting and your community, but you don't feel confident about challenging homophobia.

- You may feel some reservations about same sex couples having children, but you know you have to treat everyone equally in your practice.

- You may feel unsure how to respond when children use 'gay' as an insult or when a child teases another for playing in a way that can be seen by some as gender-inappropriate.

- You may feel that people who follow particular religions are entitled to their beliefs and that it is OK if they believe homosexuality is morally wrong.

Being able to consider all these ideas and being able to discuss them is part of reflective practice. The most important aspect of this is that the starting point must be that all practitioners feel safe enough to share their ideas. Sometimes thinking about where your ideas come from, perhaps sharing some of your own childhood experiences, can be very valuable. Lucy explains:

I grew up in a very small, conservative village in a rural part of England. I don't remember even knowing about lesbians and gay men. I think I was very naive. When I moved here and started working in this setting, I was really shocked, as one of the children had two mums. I feel ashamed now when I think about it. It was like

I didn't know how to talk to them and I was really embarrassed. I don't think they liked me, which is hardly surprising, and that just made it harder. If I'd been able to talk about it without feeling judged, it would really have helped.

Feeling free to discuss these issues, challenge assumptions and have our own assumptions challenged in relation to families with LGBT parents is a central part of reflective practice. Part of this can be to continually discuss:

- Is there anything we can do differently?
- Is there anything else we need to know?
- How can we find the information we need?
- How can we share our ideas and build on them?

These discussions can take place during staff meetings and training days, by writing ideas down in a 'reflective practice' book, using a noticeboard for ideas, by writing blogs or through informal discussion.

By thinking carefully about communication and partnerships with parents, and by building your thoughts about this into your reflective practice, you will be adding to the inclusive ethos of your setting.

Displays and resources

Chapter 7 looks in detail at resources and ideas for using them, but they deserve a mention here, as they are so vital in terms of good practice with children and families. Displays are often the first thing children and their parents will notice when they enter your setting. Try looking at your setting with fresh eyes and imagine you are a child with LGBT parents entering the setting for the first time. Is there anything around that tells the child that you value their family? For example, Stonewall (2014) produce a colourful poster with the heading 'Different Families, Same Love', which shows a range of different families, including families with same sex parents.

As well as commercially bought resources, it is worth considering if the displays within your setting reflect diversity. If you have a parents' area, are all families represented there with photographs and family news?

Do your books and other visual images reflect diversity? Does your role-play area allow for a range of families to be created, e.g. doll's house figures? Do your dressing-up clothes allow for exploration of a variety of roles for both boys and girls? As Lee stresses, the environments children spend time in are crucial in the development of an understanding of diversity:

> The early years are logically and practically a good place to start fostering and strengthening children's identities, and to raise positive awareness of diversities. It is a time when children are learning about their world from everything that is around them – their families, their peers, other people they meet, the media, their toys, books and other resources that they play with or encounter.
>
> (2007: 29)

This shows what an important area this is and conveys the responsibility that practitioners have to think carefully about resourcing and equipping their settings.

Case study 5.2

Amelia is 3 years old and lives with her adoptive fathers. She attends a pre-school four mornings a week. Amelia's keyworker has noticed another child asking Amelia about her fathers, and on one occasion heard him saying, 'My dad says it's weird to have two dads. How did you get two dads?' Amelia didn't answer and walked away. Her keyworker has realised that she doesn't feel confident dealing with this, so she has asked to discuss it with the rest of the team.

The setting is very committed to reflective practice and use team discussions as an important part of this. Amelia's keyworker tells the team about the situation and what she has overheard being said. They decide to try using a Persona Doll with the children to introduce the idea of same sex parents. They plan to buy a new persona doll and give her a life story that includes living with two mothers. They decide they don't want to make the story too close to that of Amelia, as they don't want it to be too closely focused on her (see Chapter 6 for more detail on working with Persona Dolls). One member of staff has been on training about using Persona Dolls, so she volunteers to run the session (Persona Doll Training 2014).

The whole team also think about responses that would support Amelia without undermining other children, who may express their curiosity in a way that could be hurtful to Amelia. They decide to think about ways of supporting the children to understand that there are many different families and that what matters is how you feel in your family. They think about their resources, their displays and their own responses to the children's comments.

The manager also praises Amelia's keyworker for bringing up the issue and for having the courage to admit that she didn't know how to handle the situation. The team agree that they will discuss things again in two weeks, by which time the Persona Doll will have been used with the children and other team members will have had a chance to think about what other resources or changes to displays may be appropriate.

Points to consider

- What do you notice about how the team uses reflective practice to support their work with the children?
- Do you think there is anything else they could consider?
- How do you think Amelia will respond when the Persona Doll is introduced?
- What ethos do you think the manager is trying to create when she praises Amelia's keyworker for her honesty?

Discussion

The staff at this setting are using a reflective practice cycle to help them deal with a situation that they are unfamiliar with. They have thought about changes that they want, they have considered how they will achieve this and they have planned to review these changes. This review may lead to more changes or refinements to the changes already made. They will continue to reflect and amend as needed.

You may feel they could also have involved the parents in their thoughts about how to approach questions about Amelia's family, or possibly they could have thought about the other child's curiosity in terms of adoption. Whatever approach they take, if done sensitively, Amelia is likely to feel supported and accepted if she feels that she spends her time in a setting that values her family.

There are always multiple approaches to complex situations, and an open and reflective approach is the most likely way of developing a team willing to consider all options. The manager in this setting clearly wants to create an atmosphere where these different approaches can be safely explored.

Index for Inclusion

The Index for Inclusion is a document that was developed specifically for early years practice, based on earlier versions for primary and secondary schools. The Index aims to help settings reflect on and develop their inclusive practice. The introduction to the Index states their vision of inclusion:

Inclusion is often associated with children and young people who have impairments or are seen as 'having special educational needs'. However, in the Index, inclusion is concerned with increasing the participation of all children as well as all the adults involved in a setting. It involves a detailed look at how to reduce the barriers to play, learning and participation of any child. It is about helping settings to become more responsive to the diversity of children and young people in their communities.

(Booth, Ainscow and Kingston 2006: 1)

The Index is a highly reflective process which enables all involved to think about practice with young children and their families. It also encourages participants to think about their setting in relation to the wider community of which it is part. The authors acknowledge that this is not an easy journey and can include encountering challenging ideas:

Racism, sexism, classism, homophobia, ageism and disablism share a common root in intolerance to difference and the way power is abused to create and perpetuate inequalities. The development of inclusion may involve people in a painful process of challenging their own discriminatory practices, attitudes and institutional cultures.

(Booth et al. 2006: 6)

Based around a range of indicators and questions to prompt thinking, the Index covers all aspects of inclusion in a wide and all-embracing way. Some of the indicators relevant to the issues covered in this book are:

- Everyone is made to feel welcome
- Practitioners link what happens in the setting to children's lives at home
- Activities are planned with all children in mind
- Activities develop an understanding of differences between people
- Activities discourage stereotyping
- Differences between children are used as resources to support play, learning and participation.

(Booth et al. 2006: 47–49)

Some of the questions posed which support thinking about these indicators are:

- Is the setting welcoming to all parents/carers and other members of the local community?

- Do children avoid racist, sexist, homophobic, disablist and other forms of discriminatory name-calling?

- Are significant events, such as birth, birthday or family death, given the same importance irrespective of status?

- Do practitioners treat each other with respect irrespective of their gender or sexual orientation?

- Is respect shown for all families, including lone parents/carers, same sex parents/carers, dual and multiple heritage families, large and small families?

- Are practitioners aware of each child's home cultures and family circumstances?

- Are all sections of local communities seen as a resource for the setting?

- Is there an emphasis on celebrating difference rather than conforming to a single 'normality'?

- Is diversity seen as a rich resource to support play, learning and participation rather than as a problem?

- Are differences in family structure acknowledged and celebrated?

- Are gay and lesbian people valued by the setting as part of human diversity?

- Are racist, sexist, disablist and homophobic comments and behaviour seen as aspects of bullying?

- Do stories, songs, rhymes, conversations, visits and visitors encourage children to explore backgrounds and views which are different from their own?

- Do activities develop an understanding of differences of background, culture, ethnicity, gender, impairment, sexual orientation and religion?

- Are children encouraged to pool their knowledge and experience, e.g. of families or of different countries, regions and areas or towns?

- Are discriminatory remarks used as opportunities for learning about feelings?

- Are there familiar objects and photographs in the setting from the homes of babies/young children?

- Are puppets, dolls and photographs available to explore particular situations and emotions?

- Are parents/carers and other community members used as a source of support?

(Booth et al. 2006: 50–95)

The use of the questionnaires and tick lists that the Index provides can be an extremely supportive and creative way for settings to consider their inclusive practice in relation to working with children and their LGBT parents, alongside all other aspects of good inclusive practice.

Conclusion

This chapter has asked you to consider your practice in relation to working with children and families. By considering a range of scenarios, you were encouraged to think about the challenges and complexities of inclusive practice in relation to working with families with LGBT parents. Case study 5.1, from Phoenix Nursery, will have helped you to consider the importance of good communication, partnerships with parents, reflective practice and displays and resources. The role of reflective practice was highlighted further in Case study 5.2.

A brief look at the Index for Inclusion (Booth et al. 2006) will have further enabled you to think about ways of supporting your reflective practice. The following chapter will pick up and build on some of these ideas in relation to working with colleagues.

References

Booth, T., Ainscow, M. and Kingston, D. (2006) *Index for Inclusion: Developing Play, Learning and Participation in Early Years and Childcare* [Online]. CSIE, Available at http://www.eenet.org.uk/resources/docs/Index%20EY%20English.pdf (accessed 17 July 2014).

DfE (Department for Education) (2012) *Statutory Framework for the Early Years Foundation Stage: Setting the Standards for Learning, Development and Care for Children from Birth to Five.* London: Department for Education.

Lee, P. (2007) Networking for Respect for Diversity: Experience in the Diversity in Early Childhood and Training European Network. *Early Childhood Matters,* June 2007, 108: 29–33.

Lindon, J. (2012) *Equality and Inclusion in Early Childhood.* Oxon: Hodder Education.

Meleady, C. (2014) Equality Confusion. *Nursery World,* 2 June, 14.

Nutbrown, C. and Clough, P. (2013) *Inclusion in the Early Years.* London: Sage.

Persona Doll Training (2012) *Training with a Difference to Make a Difference* [Online]. Available at http://www.persona-doll-training.org/uktraining.html (accessed 15 July 2014).

Stonewall (2014) *Primary School Resources* [Online]. Available at http://www.stonewall.org.uk/at_school/education_for_all/quick_links/education_resources/primary_school_resources/default.asp (accessed 9 July 2014).

University of Brighton (2013) *Nursery Handbook* [pdf]. University of Brighton. Available at http://staffcentral.brighton.ac.uk/xpedio/groups/Public/documents/staffcentral/doc011872.pdf (accessed 23 May 2014).

Wolpert, E. (2005) *Start Seeing Diversity. The Basic Guide to an Anti-Bias Classroom.* St Paul, MN: Redleaf Press.

6 LGBT diversity within a staff team

- A member of our staff team is gay. Should we tell him not to mention his sexuality to parents?
- Since one of our mothers revealed that she has a female partner, a few of the other parents have been excluding her and saying that it's against their religious beliefs to support her lifestyle. What should we do?
- Our nursery is very keen to be fully inclusive but is not sure how to cover the subject of sexual orientation. Can you offer some advice please?
- I have not shared my sexuality with staff in the new nursery where I work yet because I have heard the owner make a few homophobic remarks and I don't want to lose my job. Can you advise please?

(Pre-school Learning Alliance 2010)

The questions above were published on the Pre-school Learning Alliance's website in 2011 and reflect a range of issues and concerns around LGBT diversity. All of these queries will involve the manager, leader or owner of the early years setting in trying to reach a resolution to the issue. They show a range of ways that managers feel unprepared to tackle issues arising from LGBT awareness. This chapter aims to explore some of the issues that are involved and give a range of suggestions in order to support managers, leaders and team members when thinking about LGBT colleagues.

The chapter takes as its starting point the idea that the culture of the early years setting, the way that it is run, and the ethos behind it, must inevitably come in part from the leader/manager. If the setting is to promote diversity in an active way, then it needs to be the responsibility of the person in charge to engage in and encourage this practice.

It is also the responsibility for the lead person in the setting to make sure that the setting is a safe place for children and staff. By safe, we are not just talking about health and safety issues, important as they are. Here we are talking about emotional safety and this has been addressed in terms of children and parents/carers elsewhere in the book. In this chapter we are looking at the setting in terms of the safe space it can offer for staff members.

Policies

Chapter 3 referred to the legal duties of the setting; all practitioners should be aware that it is their legal responsibility to promote diversity and to create an environment that surrounds children with a positive attitude to diversity. Practitioners reading this chapter will be able to go to the policies that guide their settings practice and should be able to find a general equalities policy. Good practice around LGBT issues, however, is something more specific than this general awareness and it won't necessarily happen naturally without the active awareness and involvement of the leader of the setting. Throughout this book we talk about how this promotion can happen – through the selection of resources, the use of language and the way that activities and displays are planned and executed.

All of this needs the leader/manager of the setting to be actively engaged in promoting good practice. This may be underpinned by the leader having to examine and think about their prejudices and attitudes before they can consider spreading this good practice with the rest of the team. It may also result in having difficult conversations with some members of staff and parents. This chapter aims to outline some examples of good practice in these areas and some ideas for strategies to combat difficult situations and conversations.

We would stress that underpinning all of this work are good communication and assertion skills. There is not space in this chapter to outline the many strategies that exist for establishing or refining these skills, but there are many good resources that can help with the development of these skills.

Because LGBT practice can be a controversial issue that challenges staff and parents, it needs to be supported by very skilful use of good communication skills. Therefore we suggest that this chapter should be read from a position of assuming that these are in place.

Gender

Traditionally the early years have been a workforce area that is staffed and led by women. Over recent years this has changed slightly and recent research by Nottingham Trent and Bedfordshire universities found that men represent 12 per cent of the primary workforce and 3 per cent of the teachers in state nurseries. The figures for private and voluntary nurseries are lower still.

Dr Krishan Sood, senior lecturer at Nottingham Trent University, said:

> Good leadership and support through mentoring and explicit role clarity by head teachers and staff are good starting points to encourage males into early-years teaching. Stereotypes, perceived or real, of gender inequality, homophobia or identity need to be challenged and addressed.
>
> (Sood 2013)

This book is not intending to explore general gender issues con-nected with the early years workforce in any great depth. What can be discussed is the fact that there is a link between gender and LGBT diversity, as even a slight change in the traditional identity of the early years workforce can raise issues that are connected to LGBT diversity as well as gender. As mentioned in the quote above, there can be stereotypical attitudes from staff and parents towards men who choose to have a career in early years, and this can result in homophobia.

Well, what real man would want to work with babies and be surrounded by women all day?

(father of a pre-school child)

I haven't told the staff that I am gay – I just assume that they think it anyway, I kind of give myself away with the way I look and my voice.

(male manager of an early years creche)

In this chapter we also need to mention another important and controversial stereotype and assumption: the sometimes perceived link between gay men and paedophilia. Again, this is not the place to examine gender issues generally, but this link needs to be challenged firmly and knowledgably by staff members if it is ever raised by parents or any adult in a setting. Gregory M. Herek (2013), a researcher and writer in California, makes reference to research that shows clearly that there is no link between child molestation and homosexuality:

Members of disliked minority groups are often stereotyped as representing a danger to the majority's most vulnerable members. For example, Jews in the Middle Ages were accused of murdering Christian babies in ritual sacrifices. Black men in the United States were often lynched after being falsely accused of raping White women.

In a similar fashion, gay people have often been portrayed as a threat to children. Back in 1977, when Anita Bryant [1997] campaigned successfully to repeal a Dade County (FL) ordinance prohibiting anti-gay discrimination, she named her organization 'Save Our Children,' and warned that 'a particularly deviant-minded [gay] teacher could sexually molest children.'

(Herek 2013)

Case study 6.1

A member of staff tells you, the manager, that a parent has taken them aside and told her that she does not want L, a male member of staff who has been open with parents and staff about his sexuality, to change her baby's nappies. 'She's just not comfortable about it,' reports the child's keyworker. You suspect that the key worker agrees with the parent's view although she doesn't say this clearly to you.

What can you do?

Some suggestions would be to have a conversation with the parents in which you talk generally about the nursery's safeguarding procedures that ensure safety for both children and staff. You could then go into this in greater detail with regard to nappy-changing routines. A longer-term strategy could be to make parents more aware of all staff and their backgrounds, so that they feel reassured in regard to staff member's qualifications and experience – perhaps a 'Meet the staff member' page in the newsletter or a 'staff member of the month' feature on the noticeboard. In this way, connections of trust and parent attachment can be fostered in the same way that those between staff and children are. You would also have to think about ways to deal with the staff member who you think agrees with the parent. In this chapter we have suggested ways to make the staff team more aware of the assumptions that they are making.

Training

Talking about these assumptions, whether or not the staff team has any male staff members, is a good starting point for team meeting and in-house training. Starting to unpick the attitudes that the team have towards men working in early years is a valuable exercise in progressing to look at LGBT diversity.

Difficult conversations

The most important issue when having a difficult conversation with a colleague or parent is to set the interaction up and to do some preparation. The leader or staff member should not feel rushed into replying to a comment or dealing with a difficulty at that point where it happens if it doesn't seem appropriate. It may be that the place and time are not conducive to a thought-out and reflective discussion where people feel safe to be open and to admit liability or consider other points of view.

The conversation should take place without children or other staff members in earshot and be at a time when both people have the time and attention to be reflective. We personally think that it is also good practice to let the other person know what is going to be discussed rather than just saying to them something like, 'Can we have a chat at 4 pm, please?' This may lead to the person spending all the time leading up to the meeting wondering what the discussion might be about and therefore entering into it feeling worried, anxious and fearful, or angry, resentful and already thinking of all the ways they will refute the points made.

Case study 6.2

A group of early years staff are out at a restaurant for an evening social meal at the end of term. They are discussing some children who attend the nursery and one room leader remarks on a little boy who especially likes to dress in the sparkly sari in the dressing-up box. She is his keyworker and you overhear her commenting, 'I know that his father isn't happy with it and I don't blame him. It's odds on that he's going to grow up that way, you know.' Some of the other members of the group look uncomfortable, and one of them looks pointedly at you, waiting to see your reaction.

What can you do?

You could choose to confront the member of staff at that point and ask them, 'What do you mean by that? He might grow up to be gay? What would be wrong with that?' There are a range of outcomes here. The staff member could say that they didn't mean anything and that this is out of work time anyway and they can say what they think. They could be defensive and say that you misheard them. They could even apologise and say that it was the wine talking. The point is that you would not be prepared for this encounter, and to tackle this in such an exposed forum with the rest of the staff looking on might not be the best way to deal with the incident. Equally, the rest of the team need to know that you will talk about this in the future and that they can be reassured that their feeling that the staff member should not be talking in this way was correct.

Ways forward

One way of dealing with this is to say lightly, 'Oh, that's a topic for another discussion,' to ensure that everyone is aware that you have heard the comment and mean to challenge it at some point. Another suggestion would be to ignore the issue when it happens, but in both cases you would need to make some time at work to talk to the staff member privately and challenge them about the conversation. A starting point could be about confidentiality and discussing children and their families in such an open way in public. This could be followed up by a chat with the father concerned, so that he could air his worries and think about what he is actually worried about. Finally, it may be appropriate to arrange the next staff meeting to include some in-house training on attitudes towards LGBT issues, using the Stonewall material or ideas from this book. Again, this would give the rest of the staff team the message that such comments need discussion. They might have been made in social time, but they reveal attitudes that could impact on the nursery.

Training for staff

It is important first to establish where the majority of the staff team is in terms of understanding and attitudes, and then lead them on to a further point. In this way assumptions and attitudes that people hold can be examined and unpicked and they can be introduced to the next level or layer in thinking. This will have a higher chance of success rather than starting from a point that is very challenging and threatening to the group and may cause people to withdraw from the discussion and refuse to engage with the ideas and concepts. In order to engage with this process, it is important to be well prepared. We would suggest that delivering this training would require a confident attitude and knowledge of LGBT issues. This would mean either getting an outside person to deliver the training, from the Local Authority list of approved trainers or from Stonewall, or going on such training first and then cascading it to staff members.

Feeling unconfident about the material and not being able to respond to the challenges raised by staff members in a training session can send the wrong message to the staff team. It may seem to them that the training is only happening because it is a box that needs to be ticked rather than a whole team effort to bring everyone up to speed and provide an inclusive and supportive environment for children, parents and staff. It may seem as though the manager is paying lip service to good equalities practice rather than really understanding and wanting to improve the practice in the setting. The two phrases we often hear when delivering this type of training are 'Well, we do all of that, anyway,' and 'This is political correctness gone mad.' Being able to respond to both of those statements is an important aspect of this type of training.

Because of the content of the material, it is not as straightforward as delivering training on, for example, health and safety or even managing behaviour. Subjects like safeguarding children are emotive and a range of attitudes from colleagues can surface in training sessions. There is something about LGBT issues, though, that makes it the most sensitive and personally challenging of topics to train staff in or even discuss. The baseline is that we are not talking about sex when we are discussing sexuality and that is hard for some people to grasp, and to even start to think, that there is a need for LGBT issues to be raised in an early years setting.

It might be that unexpected information comes out at this training. Staff might reveal information about their own sexuality or that of a family member or friend. They might have some information about a parent who has spoken to them – that a child has two mothers or two fathers, for example – and the manager is unaware of this. Because of this, as a starting point it is very important that the manager doesn't make any assumptions about the staff team in regards to sexuality. Setting up an arena where they are addressing 'us', the heterosexuals, and talking about 'them', the LGBT people, will make those assumptions clear to the audience and set up a 'them and us' situation.

The staff team also needs to be able to show their unawareness of issues knowing that they will not be judged or criticised for it in such a public and exposing arena. For example, some people can think that gay men and paedophilia are closely associated and that gay men automatically have an interest in young boys.

In order for such revealing information to surface, there needs to be a supportive and nurturing environment in a setting that extends not just around the children but also around the staff and families. Staff members who hold such beliefs need to be given correct information, so that they can process this new knowledge and start to examine some of the ideas that they previously thought were fact. This needs to be done in a sensitive way that shows colleagues that such beliefs are not acceptable, because they are not true. It is hard to do this if someone's beliefs and understandings are so different from one's own and so at odds with the ethos that the manager is trying to establish in a setting. It can be tempting to be confrontational with that person and to tell them that they are wrong and should not be voicing their opinion in an early years setting.

A result of such a standoff is that person will be very unlikely to voice any of their opinions again and there would be no chance of them moving on from the belief system that they have. A suggestion that we have found helpful in many difficult situations in staff training is to start from the setting's mission statement or vision statement. If there isn't one, then a separate activity would be to write one. All staff members should be aware if there is such a statement and know that they have agreed to it and understood it, along with the policies that guide the practice of the setting. Starting with a statement that everyone present agrees with is a good basis and initial platform, which then leads on to further discussions. Working in early years often brings with it an understanding that the job also carries a signing up to certain values that are part of the 'hidden curriculum' or portfolio that early years workers agree to. It is not a job where people enter into it for large salaries, power and career advancement, status or other material perks. Generally, it is a job that people do because they like being with children and want to provide the best possible care and learning opportunities for them. It is rare that this is even spelled out or discussed. Practitioners often just feel that it is an understood moral position that is essential, and an integral part of working with young children.

This is always a good starting point for a staff team to start and to agree with. Following on from that is how we do this, how can we agree to provide this nurturing and inclusive environment, and that is where the interesting discussions begin.

Being 'out' at work

In this chapter, and in other places in the book, we have referred to someone being 'openly gay'. it might be useful to unpick this further and to think in more depth about what it might mean in terms of the early years workplace.

Individual reflective activity

Think about the staff team you work with and the personal details that you know about each member. Do they have children? Do they have a partner?

Points to consider

It might be that you know more details about some staff members' private life than others. Of course, there are many reasons for this: some people are more disposed to share personal details than others; some of the staff team may be closer to you than others and so you know more about their lives; some people may have worked there for longer, so there is more opportunity to know more about them.

Activity for a staff meeting: assumptions exercise

- Divide the team into pairs (a three is fine if you have an uneven number).

- In advance, devise a series of fun questions that staff could ask each other that reveal some personal information about each other that they may not already know. For example, 'What is this person's favourite food/drink/place to go on holiday/teen idol?' 'What did they want to be when they grew up?'

- The pairs then have to answer each question about their partner WITHOUT asking them the answer.

- They do this by relying on what they already know about their partner and also on any assumptions they make depending on the person's age, gender, class, cultural background – they guess.

- When they have both finished they show each other the answers and discuss how they arrived at them.

In our experience there is always a lot of initial resistance to doing this activity, 'why can't we just ask them the answers?', 'How are we going to get the answers? We don't know!' Once the participants understand the task they usually engage with it, and there is a lot of discussion at the end about how they arrived at their answers and which ones are right and which ones wrong. The important thing is the process – what led them to writing those answers?

If they are a close-knit staff team, the challenge for the facilitator is to ask questions that push the boundaries of what the team members might already know about each other. 'What job did they want to do when they grew up?' is an example of something they might not already know about each other. As well as a general team bonding exercise, this activity also teaches the group about assumptions and how we reach them. It shows members that it is important to have correct information, and not proceed on the basis of information that may or may not be true but that we have assumed. This is true in relationships with the children and families that use the setting as well as their interactions with each other.

Editing lives

By 'editing lives', we mean the process that a gay or trans person may go through when they are talking about their lives and thinking about how much they are willing to share in an environment that may or may not feel like a safe space. When they talk about their partners, they will skilfully avoid they use of pronouns 'he' or 'she', and say 'they' in order to make it non-gender-specific. They may say 'partner' instead of 'husband or wife' or use shorthand like 'my other half'. They may be reluctant to talk about their home life and perhaps important events such as anniversaries and celebrations. In addition, if a member of staff has transitioned, if they are trans, then they may be reluctant to talk about their own childhood if they were born into a different gender to the one that they are now.

Is it appropriate for early years staff members to talk about their sexuality?

Remember that we are talking about sexuality and not sex, and that being comfortable enough to be openly gay at work means that the staff member is happy and confident that they are valued and supported by their colleagues and management as a whole person. This must be an important state for managers and leaders to strive for – one in which everyone within a setting is able to be themselves in all aspects of their life.

Point for reflection

If you are not LGBT, imagine how it must feel to continually run information internally before it is vocalised in order to edit and censor it.

Professional image

There is a point of discussion around how much personal information staff members want to share, both at work and (perhaps more importantly) with parents and carers. They might talk in passing about holidays, birthdays, moving house, personal dietary likes and dislikes. If the member of staff has had children, they might refer to this: 'Oh, don't worry about it. My youngest took ages to learn how to brush their own teeth.' It is a good idea for a manager to think about how this exchange of information is managed and also how staff feel about it. Again, it is a good point of discussion in a staff meeting. Does being a professional mean not sharing any personal information with parents? What about confidentiality? Is there information that parents/carers should share with staff – for example, if their relationship breaks down, or if they are moving house? Is there information that we need to know in order to provide an appropriate care environment? Does this work both ways? Do parents have a right to know the carer as a person rather than just as a childcare professional?

These are all issues that should be discussed and agreed by a whole staff team, and managers and leaders should not just assume that there is unspoken agreement about such things. By making this an open discussion, an ethos of sharing and talking helps to make the setting a safe space, and someone who is gay or trans and reluctant to be open about this may feel empowered to be more honest about their lives.

Conclusion

Underpinning all of this discussion about openness and how many personal details to share is a useful theory called 'Johari's window'

(Chapman, 2003) that gives a pictorial illustration of how boundaries surrounding information are a movable issue that changes depending on the arena the individual finds themselves in. When we consider the window, we can see that what we know about ourselves and what we reveal about ourselves can move over time as we become more comfortable in our surroundings. It can also change depending on whether we are in a personal or a professional environment. There is also a section that contains what we don't know about ourselves and other people also don't know. This is an area for all of the (as yet) untapped and unknown skills that we have yet to develop. We hope that perceptive and reflective LGBT diversity work will be one of those skills.

References

Bryant, A. (1977) *The Anita Bryant Story: The Survival of Our Nation's Families and the Threat of Militant Homosexuality*. Old Tappan, NJ: Fleming H. Revell.

Chapman, A. (2003) *Johari's Window* [Online]. Available at http://www.usc.edu/hsc/ebnet/Cc/awareness/Johari%20windowexplain.pdf (accessed 19 August 2014).

Herek, Gregory (2013) *Facts About Homosexuality and Child Molestation* [Online]. Available at http://psychology.ucdavis.edu/faculty_sites/rainbow/html/facts_molestation.html (accessed 12 August 2014).

Pre-school Learning Alliance (2010) *Early Years Settings – Sexual Orientation – Q&A* [Online]. Available at https://www.pre-school.org.uk/providers/inclusion/452/early-years-sexual-orientation-q-a (accessed 22 September 2014).

Sood, K. (2013) *Strong Leadership Needed to Encourage More Males into Early Years Education* [Online]. Available at http://www.ntu.ac.uk/apps/news/135064-15/Strong_leadership_needed_to_encourage_more_males_into_early_years_education.aspx (accessed 1 September 2014).

7 Resources

When thinking about resources, it is easy to imagine that this will be a list of useful books, puzzles, toys and ideas for activities. While all those things are very important and will be considered in this chapter, first it is worth pausing to consider the idea that it is the people in a setting (children, parents and practitioners) who are the main resource.

> There are always more resources to support play, learning and participation than are currently used. Resources are not just about money. Like barriers they can be found in any aspect of a setting: in practitioners, management committee/governors, children, parents/ carers, communities, and through changes in cultures, policies and practices. Practitioners may have skills that they have not revealed or are not fully used and there may be community members who share a background . . . with a child who can help to make them feel at home. The resources in children, in their capacity to direct their own learning and play and to support each other, may be particularly under-utilised, as may the potential for practitioners to support each other's development.
>
> (Booth, Ainscow and Kingston 2006: 7)

The very best resources and the widest range of diverse images, books, dolls, puzzles and dressing-up clothes will not add up to good inclusive practice if the commitment and dedication of the people in a setting is weak. By valuing diversity yourself and acknowledging the experiences that children bring to your setting, you are making a statement about how important these resources are to you. They are not 'specialist equipment', hidden away in a cupboard for some rare occasion. They are part of your everyday practice and available to the children to explore, create and learn with. This chapter will look at ideas for using some relevant resources, but the commitment and dedication needs to come from you!

One of the authors of this book was an inspector of day care settings and saw many instances where nurseries had state-of-the-art resources and premises but struggled to provide a meaningful diverse experience for children. Other settings that were run on a shoestring and in premises of a lower standard had excellent links with the local community and a real understanding of what it means to have outstanding equalities practice within the team.

The message that we are trying to convey in this chapter is that good equalities practice, especially in regard to LGBT diversity, is not something that can be bought. Having said that, there are resources that can enhance and support practice, and we are aware that settings sometimes struggle to access them and we hope that this chapter will provide some useful direction. The most important action plan for a setting is to look at the resources that they have and also ensure that practitioners interact with those resources in an appropriate way in order to fully support children in their play.

Resourcing for equality

All children, and families, need to feel a sense of personal welcome and belonging within your setting . . . Children and their families absorb the messages communicated by the physical details of your environment: spaces, access, the range of resources and how you choose to use the potential of visual displays. Children need to be reassured that 'people like me' obviously have a place here.

(Lindon 2012: 147)

While this is clearly important, it is also useful to remember that resourcing for equality isn't simply about reflecting the children and families who use your setting; it is also about reflecting society as a whole and providing children with images of children and families who are not like them. Developing an awareness of and empathy for difference is a central aspect of good inclusive practice (see Case study 6.1)

Case study 7.1

Scenario 1

A small parent-run playgroup is welcoming a new family to the setting. The parents are a lesbian couple who have just moved into the area and chose the playgroup, as they want to get to know local families. They have a daughter who is 2 years old. One of the mums works full-time and the other is a stay-at-home mum. She wants to get involved in the playgroup and has offered to help out on a regular basis. The playgroup have had children with LGBT parents use the setting previously and they are a diverse group of practitioners used to thinking about diversity and equality. However, they are concerned that their resources do not reflect this family's structure and they want to change this.

Scenario 2

A childminder has never knowingly had any children with LGBT parents in her setting. However, she recently went on a day's training on equality and diversity and this has made her want to think more broadly about her practice. She was particularly struck by the trainer saying that good practice in this area is good practice for all. She has thought carefully about other areas of diversity for many years and has identified LGBT equality as a gap in her knowledge and provision.

Points to consider

- What could each setting think about in relation to resources?
- Are there differences in what each setting could provide?

- Do you think parents might react differently in each setting?

- Do you think it is more important for a setting with a child with LGBT parents to provide appropriate resources or do you think this is something all settings should do?

Discussion

In many ways both of these settings approach how to choose resources in the same way. They are each trying to increase the recognition of diversity. While the first setting has reached this conclusion because of a particular family joining the setting, the second setting recognises that this is an important aspect of inclusive provision. As discussed throughout this book, recognising and respecting all aspects of diversity is an important part of early years education and care.

While increasing diversity in resources is the aim of both settings, there may be minor differences in how this is approached. As the first setting is responding to a particular family, there may be specific resources that relate to that – for example, photographs of 'people who are important to us' will need to include both this child's mums. However, generally speaking, the differences in resourcing these two settings will be minimal.

There may be some differences in reaction from parents in the two settings. Some might be more accepting if they can see it relates to a specific family. This is where your policies will be very important so that you can show parents your commitment to equality and diversity includes all children and all families who currently use your setting, who may use it in the future or who are part of your community.

Ofsted

With the recent revision of the EYFS in September 2014, there is less emphasis in the actual report and inspection frameworks on inspectors making a specific judgment on the range of resources and the way that the setting uses them. There is an underpinning ethos, though, that good-quality resources, used effectively, enhance a child's experience at an early years setting. We argue that, although this practice is not listed and highlighted as a desirable outcome, it is good practice and has to underpin the outcomes that are emphasised. The use of diverse resources of all kinds needs to be in place so that all children can experience difference in a positive way. This good equalities practice has been part of quality early years practice for many years, and highlighting the LGBT aspect of this should be an adjustment of what should already be there.

Safeguarding children

We hope that the absence of emphasis on the quality and use of resources in the inspection process means that this aspect of equalities practice is assumed to be embedded in early years settings and should be a prerequisite, or a given, in every childcare facility. It should be a basic layer in the makeup of every setting rather than something that can be opted into. We note that there is an emphasis on children feeling 'safe' in a setting. This, of course, is important in terms of safeguarding children. We would argue that it can also be interpreted as making a child feel emotionally safe and protected at a setting. Ultimately children should be able to be open about their families and about their own questions regarding gender and sexuality. They should feel that staff care and listen to them and that they can feel safe talking about anything to them in the knowledge that they will be answered truthfully and thoughtfully. In order for staff to enable this, they also have to feel safe and valued in their diversity in the setting.

It can also be argued that, even with the current inspection emphasis on 'school readiness' and learning and assessment processes, diverse resources play their part in ensuring that a child feels emotionally secure and valued and confirmed in their experiences and background. In this way the selection and use of appropriate resources will only enhance a child's experiences. These experiences may be a direct reflection and affirmation of their own family life, or they may be a window into the rich and diverse backgrounds of those children and adults in the world around them. Either way, they help the child understand and be part of the society that they will enter into.

The Office for National Statistics (ONS) says that, 480,000 (1 per cent) of the people who fed back to them consider themselves gay or lesbian, and 245,000 (0.5 per cent) saw themselves as bisexual (Guardian 2010). Interestingly, Stonewall feel that these figures will increase as people get used to being asked about their sexual identity, and that asking people this question on their doorstep or over the phone may deter people who are not open about their identity from revealing it.

The EYFS and the inspection process should reflect the society that children and families are part of, and LGBT diversity is clearly part of that society and should be included in the experience of a child. Resources are part of providing that experience in an appropriate way that reflects and supports the child's own interests and play. In the current inspection process we would argue that resources that show LGBT diversity in the activities and play of children are reflected in good practice judgments. This is especially highlighted when making a quality judgment about safety and also emotional school readiness.

Examples of reports

In the previous version of the EYFS an example of an inspection report for an Outstanding setting said:

There is a highly impressive sense of celebration of individuality throughout the nursery. On every wall, positive images celebrate individuals, families, their countries and their different languages. Children learn how to greet their friends in different languages and learn about the different culture and customs of their friends and families. Staff foster this sense of individual worth very well and as a result, all children thrive and flourish, feeling confident and special.

A nursery that was not classified as Outstanding, although working towards it, had this comment in its report:

Children have access to a wide range of challenging resources although there are fewer that show positive images of diversity.

The action plan for this latter nursery would be to ensure that they did have a wide and diverse range of resources and should include those that provide positive images of families where some members may include LGBT people. It can be seen from this that the provision of resources and activities that promote and support diversity was one that the inspection process singled out as worthy of mention.

A 2014 current Ofsted report where a provision has been inspected to the more recent version of the EYFS describes an Outstanding setting as follows:

Practitioners have very high expectations of themselves and the children. Using their expert knowledge of the areas of learning and a clear understanding of how children learn they provide rich, varied and imaginative experiences for the children.

Resources and diversity are not explicitly mentioned, but it is apparent that the effective provision and use of resources underpins this provision of rich, varied and imaginative experiences for children.

The current guidelines for Ofsted inspectors draw their attention to making a judgment on how well the setting fulfils its role in the following areas.

How well teaching strategies, together with support and intervention, match individual children's needs and ensure that they make good progress (HM Government 2014).

Again, resources are not specifically listed, but they are part of the package of provision that would ensure that support and intervention was provided for children in order to help them progress. All of this information was taken from the Ofsted website (https://www.gov.

uk/government.publications/conducting-early-years-inspections) and is openly available. We have not included direct references to these reports, as we want to preserve the confidentiality of the settings.

Books

One of the main messages we want to convey in this section is the importance of using interesting and stimulating age-appropriate books that just happen to have LGBT characters in them. We have reservations about 'message' books where the whole emphasis is on the fact that there are same sex parents and the story is laboured and not interesting for young children. There is also the issue that many books featuring LGBT diversity are imported and therefore expensive. We would advise getting such books from a library or local resource centre.

When buying, our best advice is to look at the range offered by Letterbox Library as listed in Appendix 1. They have a very good selection of age-appropriate books. We would also recommend the guide to LGBTQ books written by B. J. Epstein (2013).

One book led the ILEA (Inner London Education Authority) to be mentioned in Parliament, as they held a copy of Susanne Bösche's *Jenny Lives with Eric and Martin* (1983) as part of their resources for teachers. This book was definitely a 'message' book that showed a young child who had two dads. It caused outrage at the time, mainly because there was a scene that showed the two dads in bed and the young girl trying to wake them up to make her breakfast because she is bored. Not an uncommon occurrence and certainly one that is explored much further in books by authors such as Babette Cole, who has a picture of a naked couple with the caption, 'Why do mummy and daddy lock me out of the bedroom' (Jennet 2010: 5). Bösche's book, which was only available for adults to select as a resource, caused a storm of protest in 1986.

The images and language that are used in books that contain LGBT characters relate to domestic arrangements – the sort of arrangements that feature in every child's book. Who lives with who, where do they sleep, who makes the meals, who helps with the homework; ordinary mundane background details that form part of the main story of the book. Such is the worry of having gay or lesbian parents in this role that often it is these arrangements that are the main focus of the book, like *Asha's Mums* (Elwin and Paulse 1990) or *Heather Has Two Mommies* (Newman 1989). Sometimes the parents are replaced by animals so as to remove any link with possible sexual activity – for example, *And Tango Makes Three* (Richardson and Parnell 2006), where the three are all penguins.

Another important point made by Jenet (2010) is that gay and lesbian characters have to be 'super' parents. They have to outshine any expectation of parental role in order to earn their right to be in a children's book. Unlike other heterosexual parents in children's books, they are always there to help with homework, listen to troubles and cook a nutritious meal.

It is only recently that we have started seeing some books that have two mums or two dads, where this is not mentioned as part of the plot. Beth Cox, founder and manager of Inclusive Minds, comments:

> We need to see same-sex families and LGBT people in an incidental way. As just part of the landscape, one of many families in the background in a school or street scene, through a window, or in a child's drawing. Great examples of this can be found in *The Lost Stars*, *The Cloud* and *Tilly's at Home Holiday* all published by Child's Play and *Jellybean goes to School* published by Random House. We're also treated to a range of LGBT characters in the scenery in lots of Bob Graham books. This is a simple way of making same-sex families and couples familiar to children and can be easily achieved by an illustrator. However this isn't enough. If diverse families are only depicted on the margins and in the background it gives the message that those families aren't as valid as others. Families headed by LGBT parents also need to star in books. Not specialist books about the many different types of family but funny, touching, exciting, heart-warming, original, but most importantly, mainstream books about families that just happen to feature two parents of the same sex rather than the opposite sex. These are the books that we need most desperately.
>
> (Cox 2014)

We would also add that such books need to explore diversity further and include more intersectionality. Books can include more than one 'issue' at a time and there can be LGBT characters who have a disability or who are ethnically diverse. We make this point in Chapter 2 when we talk about stereotyping and multiple identities. Books that just show LGBT characters as linear and only defined by being LGBT do not reflect the reality and complexity of the world that children see about them. In consequence, the books will appear lacking in a three-dimensional view of the world, and the result of this is that these people in the book will be lifeless and unreal.

A final point about books is that it is in YA (young adult) fiction where LGBT characters seem to be written in as central to the action but not part of an 'issue'. We hope that this trend will soon spread downwards in the age range and that publishers will be brave enough to commission pre-school picture books that follow this example. Perhaps after you have read this you will feel empowered to go away and write and/or illustrate such a book!

Imaginative play, dressing up and the home corner

We have mentioned the dressing-up box previously in this book and it is often the starting point of conversations about diversity. One of the most quoted examples is that of the little boy who is insistent that he wants to wear dresses and sparkly mules and whose parents are concerned.

This discussion is part of a wider one about gender, which does not belong here, but it is often misinterpreted by parents and practitioners as a sign that the child will 'grow up to be gay'. The answer to this anxiety is that he may or may not be gay when he grows up. All he is doing at the moment is exploring what it might be like to wear the clothes he has seen some adults wear. He might also be drawn to the particular colours and textures of the items that he has chosen. They may be sparkly and glittery and catch his eye. He will have seen his other friends try them on and wants to share their experience. These are just some of the reasons why the little boy is wearing what are traditionally thought of as 'female clothes'. It doesn't mean that he is starting the journey that will result in him exploring transitioning to the opposite gender or becoming 'trans'. Or it may do.

What we are saying here is that good equalities practice, in relation to LGBT diversity as it is in relation to all other elements of diversity, is to let children freely explore a wide range of experiences. There are no specific issues relating to LGBT diversity in connection with dressing-up clothes and home corners. Good equalities practice that is sensitive to gender should also support LGBT diversity.

The dressing-up box will include a selection of different clothes to try on, and the home corner will have a wide range of domestic articles that are culturally diverse. Boys and girls should be able to freely take part in and explore all aspects of these experiences, and any suggestion that it is not appropriate for them, made by members of staff or other children, should be challenged.

One point that does relate specifically to LGBT diversity concerns the home corner. As we have detailed earlier in the book, 'home' and 'family' can be interpreted in a variety of different ways. Practitioners should not impose their own cultural stereotypes on the use of home corner resources – for example, not all families use a kettle to boil water and some families may use chapatti pans or woks to cook food. In the same way, children may use the resources in the home corner to refer to their family grouping – 'This is where Mummy and Mama sleep' – and staff should be sensitive enough to not automatically correct the child with 'Don't you mean Mummy and Daddy?' This issue is covered in detail in Chapter 4, especially in the 'What's in a name?' section.

We point out the relevance to LGBT diversity here, but really this is also true of all children. Many of the families in the setting will have intricate structures: 'I live with my mum and stepdad. His two children visit us at weekends and I also have a brother who has a different dad from me.' Younger children will not be able to vocalise this so well and their explanation of their family's structure will be revealed in their play. Practitioners must be alert at all times to support and confirm the child's identity, and this includes families with parents who are LGBT.

Case study 7.2

Grace is 4 years old and attends a nursery. Her keyworker, Erica, is aware that Grace prefers to play outdoors and is happiest on the tricycles, going round and round the marked roads that are in the play area. Her other favourite activity is playing on the slide. Erica was concerned when Grace started the nursery, when she was 3 years old, that she didn't engage in more creative activities. She has now realised that, as long as those activities are outside, Grace is happy to express the more artistic side of her character.

Erica has seen other members of staff trying to engage Grace with the toys and activities in the outside home corner. One person in particular keeps trying to put a baby doll in the front part of Grace's tricycle and repeatedly offers Grace a buggy to push round when Grace has made it very clear that she has no interest in them. Erica has heard Grace being referred to as a 'tomboy' in staff meetings and, as the keyworker, she wonders if she should have a chat with Grace's parents.

Points to consider

- Should Erica talk to the parents and if so what should she say?

- Should Erica talk to the member of staff who keeps trying to engage Grace in the home corner activities?

Discussion

It is important to ask why there is any concern here rather than assume that there must be. If we examine this closely it may be that the member of staff is worried that Grace is not engaging in the activities she thinks are gender-appropriate for Grace. This relates to the assumptions exercise that we pinpointed as useful for staff teams to engage in. The discussion that staff could have should centre on questions such as 'What are "boys" activities and what are "girls"?' and, more fundamentally, 'Should there even be those divisions?' We believe that children should be free to choose from a range of play activities, and as practitioners we should not have any part in steering them towards those we feel are gender-appropriate: 'If a child engages in activities that we as adults think of as belonging to the opposite gender, does that have implications for the child's sexuality?'

The answer to this is as first stated in this section. It may, or it may not. In either case, as early years practitioners our job is to ensure that all children can freely choose activities, especially around such loaded gender areas such as the home corner and dressing-up area.

Persona Dolls

The innovative Persona Doll approach encourages children to develop empathy and challenge discrimination and unfairness. It helps counter the prejudices and misinformation they pick up even if they have no personal contact with Black and mixed parentage families, with lesbian, gay, Traveller, or refugee families or with families in which adults or children are disabled. And they absorb these negative attitudes whether they live in small villages with mainly White adults and children, in middle class leafy suburbs or in run-down inner city areas.

(Persona Doll Training 2014)

As this suggests, using Persona Dolls, as with all resources, is about developing good practice for all the children in your setting and not about targeting provision at specific children. Lindon suggests that 'These special dolls . . . can be used in a gentle way with children to help them explore the perspectives of people who appear different to themselves' (2012: 171). While difference is a crucial aspect of working towards inclusive practice and children are undoubtedly curious about difference, it is also important to support children in developing their awareness of ways in which we are the same. The central importance of working with Persona Dolls is about supporting children in their ability to develop empathy and to understand that name calling or excluding children from play is hurtful.

When starting out with using Persona Dolls, it is best if someone in the setting has had training, but if this is not possible there are resources and ideas available on the Persona Doll website (2012), which also gives links to other useful resources such as books, posters and the dolls themselves.

Davies explains that the strength of Persona Dolls is that children readily accept them and that this gives a powerful means to explore and confront inequality. She suggests that a Persona Doll can be a very useful way of introducing the issues of a child having LGBT parents. The most important thing is that 'the first time the children meet the persona doll should be a very positive experience, as if they are welcoming a new member to the class' (2010: 23).

Introducing a new Persona Doll usually takes place as part of circle time. The doll is introduced to the children and they are told about the doll's life story. It is important that all staff agree on the life story and name of the doll, so that they can all work with the doll and support the children's questions. The member of staff will speak in their normal voice and convey the thoughts and ideas between the children and the doll. If a direct question is asked of the doll, the doll will 'whisper' in the practitioner's ear, who will then pass on the answer to the group.

The life story can be any that fits with the purpose of using the doll. For example, you might develop a life story for a doll called James who lives with his two mothers and has a younger sister called Jenny. They also have a dog called Fluff, who likes to chase balls when James throws them! By creating a whole story for the doll, the children may focus on many aspects of James's life and might ask questions about his dog! They may well also ask about James having two mothers, and the practitioner needs to be prepared to answer in an honest and straightforward way.

Small world toys

Children love to play with small world toys. Unlike other aspects of imaginative role play, where the child becomes one character, with small world play, the child can be a host of characters and can act out a whole scenario rather than one role within it. The sense of agency this gives the child is a very important aspect of the child experiencing power. The opportunity to explore in this way is crucial to the developing child.

Many early years settings will be familiar with the popularity of the fire engine, the hospital, the farm, the zoo, the doll's house and many other small world resources. What all of these resources have in common is that they are populated by people. Play people come in many different varieties and there have been many improvements over recent times so that people with disabilities and people from a range of cultures are included. While children can use these people to act out situations that are familiar to them, and explore situations beyond their current experience, there may be frustrations that 'family' sets of play people are very limited in their makeup. Most companies sell sets of dolls that include a grandfather, a grandmother, a mother, a father, a girl and a boy. Some have more children and include a baby (Arc 2014; Early Years Resources 2014; Hope Educational 2014). While it may be sometime before an educational supplier sells a set of play people with same sex parents, one way round this would be to provide sufficient play people for a child to group them together in a way that is meaningful for them.

Case study 7.3

Chrissy is 3 years and 10 months old. She has been attending her early years setting since she was just 2, and the setting knows her family well. Her older brother also attended the setting before starting school. Her mothers are actively involved in the setting, although less so as the children have got older and they have increased their working hours. Chrissy loves the small world toys and often plays long and involved games with them. She is less interested in the animals, but particularly likes any play involving people. She spends a long time arranging them in groups and often talks as she plays. Her keyworker has heard her explaining to other children that this (a group of people) is her family. Her keyworker noticed that she was using two female figures to represent her parents but that she had 'borrowed' one from an Asian family set which is not representative of her family. The practitioner discussed this at a meeting and a decision was made to order more people in order to give Chrissy the options she needs to accurately reflect her family.

Points to consider

- What are your reactions to this scenario?

- What might have happened if the keyworker had not overheard Chrissy talking about her play?

- What other factors might need to be thought about to ensure Chrissy can explore and develop her play?

Discussion

As we have said throughout this book, considering and reflecting upon your reactions to these issues is central to good inclusive practice. Possibly you might feel that Chrissy was managing to represent her family in a way that satisfied her and there was not an issue. However, considering the issues more deeply is important. It would not be acceptable to only have white play people and assume a black child was happy to represent their family with these figures.

The team at this setting have responded to this issue and ordered more people so that all the children have greater flexibility. The setting might need to look at all their resources to check that they reflect the diversity of the society of which we are all part. It might also be worth involving Chrissy's mothers in the discussion about resources.

Displays, posters and anything else

This section carries on the idea that has underpinned this entire chapter. The displays and images that are visible around a setting should reflect the rich diversity of society and the experiences of children. Children's family life should be celebrated and acknowledged in whatever form it exists, and the pictures and posters around the room (that have not been produced by children) should also do this. A child who has two mums should be able to see their own pictures of their life, and also commercially produced images if they are used in the setting. In this way their experiences are validated and valued by the setting. Items such as jigsaws and other puzzles should be treated in the same way as books when thinking about diversity and inclusion. Commercially produced images used by settings convey a strong message and should be examined critically and changed regularly to ensure variety. The dominant displays in a setting should be of children's work, but we recognise that many settings have supplementary images that they display.

The more that settings ask manufacturers to produce such diverse images, the increased likelihood that they will be become more mainstream. We return to the question that we posed at the beginning of the book that some people asked us when we started this work: 'Why should little children come into contact with LGBT diversity?' One of the answers is: 'Because it is all around them in their everyday lives and the setting reflecting this visually is just an affirmation of images that they are already encountering.'

Five year olds need to be taught that gay people exist. Some five year olds will already know this; there are children in our schools today who are being brought up by parents in a same sex relationship, and there are children who have gay uncles and aunts, gay brothers and sisters, gay grandparents. There are children living next door to gay people and children whose parents socialise with gay people. Gay people pop up on television programmes like *Coronation Street*, *Hollyoaks* and *Emmerdale*. Gay people are in fact everywhere . . . except in the National Curriculum, and certainly not visibly in our schools.

(Atkinson and DePalma 2010: xi)

References

Arc (2014) *Arc Educational Supplies: Dolls and Doll's Houses* [Online]. Available at http://www.arc-education.co.uk/dolls-dolls-houses/chinese-asian-doll-family.html (accessed 24 August 2014).

Atkinson, E. and DePalma, R. (2010) *Undoing Homophobia in Primary Schools.* Stoke on Trent: Trentham Books.

Booth, T., Ainscow, M. and Kingston, D. (2006) *Index for Inclusion: Developing Play, Learning and Participation in Early Years and Childcare* [Online]. Available at http://www.eenet.org.uk/resources/docs/Index%20EY%20 English.pdf (accessed 17 July 2014).

Bösche, S. (1983) *Jenny Lives with Eric and Martin.* London: Gay Men's Press.

Cox, B. (2014) *Making Pre-school Inclusion a Reality* [Online]. Available at http://www.publishers.org.uk/index.php?option=com_content&view=articl e&id=2776:guest-blog-making-pre-school-inclusion-a-reality&catid =499:general&Itemid=1608 (accessed 22 September 2014).

Davies, L. (2010) *Out for our Children. Foundation Stage Pack.* London: Out For Our Children.

Early Years Resources (2014) *Early Years Resources: Wooden and Plastic Figures* [Online]. Available at http://www.earlyyearsresources.co.uk/imaginative-play-c13/miniature-world-figures-c22 (accessed 24 August 2014).

Elwin, R. and Paulse, M. (1990) *Asha's Mums.* Toronto: Women's Press.

Epstein, B. (2013) *Are the Kids All Right?* London: HammerOn Press.

Guardian (2010) UK Gay, Lesbian and Bisexual Population Revealed [Online]. http://www.bbc.co.uk/news/uk-11398629 (accessed 13 August 2014).

HM Government (2014) *Inspecting early years providers – guidance for inspectors,* [Online]. Available at https://www.gov.uk/government/publications/ conducting-early-years-inspections (Accessed 19 March 2015)

Hope Educational (2014) *Hope Educational: Small World Play* [Online]. Available at http://www.hope-education.co.uk/productlist/Small-World/ Small-World-Play (accessed 24 August 2014).

Jenet, M. (2010) Why Do It? In E. Atkinson and R. DePalma (eds), *Undoing Homophobia in Primary Schools.* Stoke on Trent: Trentham Books.

Lindon, J. (2012) *Equality and Inclusion in Early Childhood.* Oxon: Hodder Education.

Newman, L. (1989) *Heather Has Two Mommies.* New York: Alyson Books.

Persona Doll Training (2012) *Training with a Difference to Make a Difference* [Online]. Available at http://www.persona-doll-training.org/uktraining.html (accessed 15 July 2014).

Richardson, J. and Parnell, P. (2006) *And Tango Makes Three.* New York: Simon and Schuster Children's Books.

8 | Conclusion

When we began researching for this book it became apparent that there was very little published material that solely addressed the issues of LGBT diversity in early years practice. We found a lot of material that focuses on the older age range, both primary and secondary. The emphasis of this work is often on tackling homophobic bullying and recognising that children live in all kinds of families. What is different in early years is that working with those families as well as the children is a far more central aspect than it is in later years of education.

We also found that, of the books that focus on issues of equality and inclusion in early years, most give a few pages (if any) to LGBT diversity. While those that mention it do so in a positive and encouraging way, we felt the issues deserved a book of their own, where there was space to explore the ideas in more depth. We have set this within the context of general good inclusive practice.

We also felt that it was important to take some space in the book to look at staffing issues. In order to support this work with children, staff members who define themselves as LGBT need to feel that the workplace is a safe and supportive environment for them. If they are able to freely be themselves, then the children and families who use the setting will see a positive role model of LGBT diversity. In terms of the relationship with parents, we wanted also to focus on the needs of the families who use the setting where members of that family define themselves as LGBT, so that they would be fully aware that they could make reference to their lives freely and know that their child's individual background would be referred to, respected and celebrated. It is crucial that children, practitioners and families don't feel that this aspect of their lives needs to be 'edited out'. For us LGBT diversity is a holistic issue that has relevance to the children, families, practitioners and management of a setting and should be apparent in every aspect of practice in order to normalise this aspect of diversity and not see it as an isolated 'issue'.

We feel passionately that early years practitioners have to respect the adult that the child will be and help to prepare them for the future. There is a lot of emphasis on 'school readiness' at the moment. We also believe in 'life readiness', and for us part of that is ensuring that the full range of possibilities in terms of sexual identity are acknowledged and reflected in the setting.

Good practice

Throughout this book, we have asked you to consider a range of aspects of early years practice that could be connected to LGBT diversity. In order to support you with this we have tried to give you an overview of the legislation connected with LGBT rights, both in the UK and internationally.

We have also raised some issues that directly concern LGBT diversity and the families where one or more people may be LGBT. We have been very specific about the use of language and firmly believe that such precise definitions are necessary. This is because, historically, LGBT people have had, and continue to have, strong associations with a range of negative and pejorative comments that are linked to their sexuality in a way that heterosexual people do not have. As a recent example, and to emphasise this, we ask you to think of the widespread use of the word 'gay' as a negative term in playgrounds around the country.

We are aware that there will be early years practitioners who believe that children, especially very young ones, should not be linked in any way to LGBT diversity. We hope that this book has supported the message that we are not talking about sex when we refer to sexuality or gender choice. We are talking about the makeup of families and society. We make the point strongly that children are surrounded by

LGBT diversity in their everyday life through images and references in the media and connections through their families and friends. It is only in education, and especially early years education, that there is no mention at all.

We believe that early years should reflect the rich and varied mix of life that children encounter and that LGBT diversity is part of that mix.

We hope that the case studies and examples we have given you will provide inspiration and reassurance that LGBT people are part of life. This aspect of diversity should be approached in the same way as any other category of diversity and, eschewing categories completely, it should also just be part and parcel of children's everyday lives rather than issues focused.

Leading on from this ethos, we hope that Chapter 7, on resources, shows that the most effective use of books and other play-based materials is underpinned by an adherence to the idea of LGBT as a family's ordinariness, rather than a special problem that needs to be supported and solved with specific resources that wouldn't be used by any other child.

The activities that we include are suitable starting points for staff teams to initiate discussions and think around LGBT diversity. We hope that this book will provide a springboard for interesting and thoughtful training sessions in colleges, universities, schools and early years settings. We are aware of the sensitivity of this material, and feel that in order to deliver this kind of training there needs to be an understanding of good communication skills and a supportive staff ethos where people can speak freely and honestly and feel able to own the statements they make. In this way, any worries and fears team members may have can be discussed and resolved in a meaningful way.

Looking to the future

Internationally, LGBT diversity is not celebrated and recognised universally. We have looked at the United Nations Convention on the Rights of the Child and noted that, while most countries have signed up to this, many of those countries outlaw homosexuality. Of those that don't actually outlaw same sex relationships, there are countries, such as Russia, that have shown recently that they have a very negative attitude towards being gay, and there are places where being openly LGBT can be a very dangerous decision. Those people who choose to openly declare their sexuality in these circumstances show great courage.

In contrast to this there have been great strides forward in recent years in terms of equality for people who identify as LGBT in the UK. Recent legislative changes mean that, in a legal sense at least, there are protections and safeguards against discrimination and homophobia. The last half-century has seen a change from homosexual acts being criminal to marriage equality. While it may not have seemed so to those experiencing discrimination, this is a relatively fast rate of change and there is some evidence that not everyone in society has caught up with or adapted to these changes.

Consequently, homophobia is still a real and frightening part of everyday life for many in the LGBT community. Legal changes do not always equate with a change in attitudes, and away from the big cities of London, Manchester and Brighton there are places in the UK where being openly gay while also raising children can be an isolating and difficult experience. Some families may choose to deny living in a same sex relationship or decide not to apply to be adoptive parents because of the attitudes of the other parents in their communities. If they see that their local early years settings do not provide an inclusive welcome that involves LGBT diversity, they would feel even more reluctant to share their lives with the setting. The setting may then not be privy to crucial information about the child and their family. We have written this book with those families in mind and hope that the ideas and information that we are providing to practitioners will help make it possible for those families to be recognised and supported and to be able to be honest about their family structure.

In addition to that, we cannot overstress that LGBT diversity should be part of a child's package of experiences in the early years and no different to any other recognition of diversity. Even without any parents or carers who identify as LGBT, or any staff members who do the same, the setting has a duty to show their children the wider world.

Possibilities

Working with children in the early years is about possibilities. We have evidence of this from the Sure Start programme, which understood that resources put into children's services and family support in the first five years of a child's life would be repaid in later years, as that child would stand a better chance of not being part of the numbers of young people with unwanted pregnancies or who were involved in drug taking or in contact with the law enforcement system.

This is consistent with research showing links between parenting and educational achievement, behaviour problems, criminality and violence, teenage pregnancy, drug and alcohol misuse, and mental and physical health. There was also growing evidence that parenting could mediate the effects of deprivation on outcomes later in life, and therefore support for parenting was an essential part of efforts to reduce child poverty (Barlow et al. 2007).

We feel that as part of this work good equalities practice gives the underpinning message to children and families that they are respected and valued. LGBT diversity is crucial because it is a pledge to the future. An early years setting doesn't know which families have chosen not to use their facility because they couldn't see their own lives reflected in the setting's environment. They have no idea how many practitioners have not applied for jobs there because they felt that they wouldn't be supported. Finally, they have no idea of the future sexual identities of the young children that they care for, and there is every likelihood that a significant number of them will grow up and explore their sexuality and then think of themselves within the LGBT definition.

Throughout this book we have tried not to make assumptions about the reader. We don't want this book to sound as though we are only addressing a heterosexual reader and giving them a window on a previously unknown area of practice. People reading this book will have different levels of experience and understanding of LGBT issues. We are fully aware that there are practitioners, students, childcare and education professionals, and other interested people, who define as LGBT, and we hope that our voice includes them as well. We feel that everyone has something to learn from the discussion, questions, information and case studies that we have presented, whatever their sexuality or identity.

We know that the experiences that we have when young can shape, define and influence our future selves. We ask you to think about the pre-school manager we interviewed when researching this book who felt that Section 28 influenced his teenage years so negatively, as teachers were cautious about being seen as 'promoting homosexuality' and were unable to support him. In contrast, imagine a young person who is able to look back at their early years and remember it as a time when LGBT diversity was recognised as part of life; where their future sexuality was not treated as something that was shameful or needed to be hidden away, but as a valid lifestyle and that having children, by whatever means, could be part of that life. The numbers of young people who take their own lives because of feelings of shame about being gay or trans are unacceptable.

Nearly one in four (23 per cent) lesbian, gay and bisexual young people have tried to take their own life at some point. Girls are more likely to attempt this than boys (29 per cent compared to 16 per cent). Gay young people who experience homophobic bullying are much more likely to attempt to take their own life than gay young people who aren't bullied; 28 per cent have attempted to take their own life compared to 17 per cent. Seven in ten (71 per cent) lesbian and bisexual girls and almost six in ten (57 per cent) gay and bisexual boys have thought about taking their own life, with boys who are black or minority ethnic at particular risk of suicidal thoughts, at 76 per cent. Gay young people who experience homophobic bullying are much more likely to think about taking their own life (72 per cent compared to 56 per cent). In comparison, the Samaritans say that 7 per cent of all young people in general have ever attempted to take their own life and 20 to 45 per cent have thought about it (Guasp and Taylor 2012).

As a society we should be doing everything we can to alleviate this suffering. We feel that a supportive early years environment where being LGBT is discussed and confirmed must send the right message to young people, even if they are not getting this message in their own families – especially important if they are not getting this in their home environment. This early years work sets the scene for good diversity foundations and can be crucial in later years as a confirmation that whoever a child is, they will be celebrated and loved.

Working in early years education and care is a vitally important part of this slow but steady move to true equality. Young children are the most accepting and open age group in society and, therefore, early years practitioners are well placed to start thinking about working for equality. While it is certainly true that young children are curious about difference, it is also true that they are accepting and respectful of those differences when given the information they need and the opportunity to explore without judgment.

We are not pretending that it is easy to confront challenging issues. It can be hard challenging yourself, and it can be even harder challenging others. The No Outsiders project aims to present just such challenges and to show ways of meeting them. Atkinson and DePalma state its aim as being:

> not simply to address homophobic bullying but to *undo* homophobia at source, by challenging heteronormativity – the assumption that the world and everything in it is, and should be, based on a heterosexual model – and by challenging heterosexism – the privileging of heterosexual identities and relationships over all others.
>
> (2010: ix, emphasis in original)

Although the project mainly focused on primary schools, one nursery setting took part in the project. A practitioner in that setting describes how difficult it was to confront some of the homophobia they encountered but how positive it was to see that change over time. She tells how one father found it very hard that a poster in the setting showed a range of different families, including a child with two fathers. Through careful discussion about what things might be hard for a child to live with and what things a child needs to thrive, he began to question his assumptions and beliefs. He began to realise that a lot of his beliefs were based on stereotypes. Slowly he saw the connection between his own beliefs and how those beliefs get passed on to the children. The value of what they were trying to achieve in this project started to become evident to him.

This is what this book is for. By working through the challenges you meet, you will slowly but surely be part of a movement for change – not only towards a more tolerant society, but towards one where differences are valued equally and all sexualities and gender identities are treated with respect.

As we have stressed elsewhere in this book, children are not born with prejudices. Prejudices, and the discrimination that leads from them, are learned. Children would not naturally be homophobic. This, too, is learned. Early years practitioners are very well placed to help support the development of respectful and open-minded children and young people. This can't be achieved without practitioners making a commitment to reflective practice and to thinking deeply about the issues discussed in this book.

We have argued throughout this book that working for LGBT equality and inclusion is part and parcel of good inclusive practice.

We end this book with a poem that was written by 7-year-old Becky, to be read out at an informal commitment ceremony between her mothers. The poem shows the easy acceptance of Becky towards this family celebration, and the poem would not necessarily have been any different if the celebration was between a woman and a man. Nearly 20 years later, Becky tells us:

No child makes up prejudice on their own, it is learned. The only time I felt different was when other people pointed out the difference in my family. It was their views rather than anything to do with my family that was sometimes hard. The effects of feeling different to everyone around you can be huge for a young child if the adults around them don't encourage honest and open discussion of it.

When I first met Mary I was very scared and shy.
But now I really love her, so I really don't know why.

I love it when she hugs me when I'm crying lots of tears.
I'm looking forward to being her daughter for years and years and years.

I really love my family and that includes the cat,
We are all extremely happy and we hope it stays like that.

References

Atkinson, E. and DePalma, E. (2010) Introducing the No Outsiders Project. In E. Atkinson and R. DePalma (eds), *Undoing Homophobia in Primary Schools*. Stoke on Trent: Trentham Books.

Barlow, J., Kirkpatrick, S., Wood, D., Ball, M. and Stewart-Brown, S. (2007) [Online]. *Family and Parenting Support in Sure Start Local Programmes*. Available at http://www.scie-socialcareonline.org.uk/family-and-parenting-support-in-sure-start-local-programmes/r/a11G00000017tBalAl (accessed 25 September 2014).

Guasp, A. and Taylor, J. (2012) *Mental Health: Stonewall Health Briefing* [Online]. Available at http://www.stonewall.org.uk/documents/mental_health.pdf (accessed 25 September 2014).

Appendix 1
Children's books

This list includes a range of books that are useful for using with children to support your work around LGBT diversity. Some specifically include the theme of children having LGBT parents, while others are a useful resource for exploring family diversity more generally. Try to avoid seeing these as specialist books that you may consider getting if you have a child in your setting who has LGBT parents. Like with all other aspects of diversity, these books should be available to all children, to widen their understanding of the diverse culture of which we are all part and to broaden their understanding of family life in all its diversity.

We are grateful to Letterbox Library, the Early Childhood Project, Out For Our Children and B. J. Epstein for help with compiling this list.

Argent, H. (2007) *Josh and Jaz Have Three Mums:* London: BAAF.

Josh and Jaz are adopted and have two mums. When they have to make a family tree at school, they decide to include their birth family, too.

Branned, S. (2008) *Uncle Bobby's Wedding.* New York: G.P. Putnam.

Chloe loves her Uncle Bobby and is worried that she won't be so close to him once he gets married. Then she realises that she won't be losing an uncle, she'll be gaining one.

Carter, V. (2007) *If I Had One Hundred Mummies.* London: Onlywomen Press.

100 mummies means multiple goodnight kisses, hugs and games. But would 100 mummies leave enough room for their little girl? Perhaps

two is, after all, the perfect number. Ideal for exploring diverse families.

Combs, B. (2001) *ABC – A Family Alphabet Book*. Ridley Park, PA: Two Lives Press.

A is for awake! A little girl is the first to be awake but not for long, as she jumps on her mums' bed loudly playing a musical instrument!

de Hann, L. and Stern, N. (2002) *King and King*. Berkeley, CA: Tricycle Press.

Like in many traditional fairy tales, it is time for the prince to marry. After many princesses are paraded in front of him, it is a prince he falls in love with and whom he marries. They then become kings.

de Hann, L. and Stern, N. (2004) *King and King and Family*. Berkeley, CA: Tricycle Press.

In this follow-on to *King and King*, the kings now adopt a little girl.

Ewart, M. (2008) *10,000 Dresses*. New York: Stories Press.

Bailey loves to wear dresses and does not get support from family. They think Bailey should avoid girlish things. Bailey does, however, get support from a friend.

Garden, N. (2004) *Molly's Family*. New York: Farrar Straus and Giroux.

Molly draws a picture of her family – Mommy, Mama Lu and Sam the puppy. Another child at her nursery says her family isn't real. This story shows that families can be different while still being loving and happy.

Griffiths, J. and Pilgrim, T. (2007) *Picnic in the Park*. London: BAAF.

By telling the story of Jason's birthday party, all his guests are introduced, including children with a range of families. Some are adopted, some have two mums or dads . . . The book includes pages at the back for children to draw their own family.

Hoffman, M. (2010) *The Great Big Book of Families*. London: Frances Lincoln Children's Books.

A glorious, multicultural celebration of contemporary family life. Includes lesbian/gay parents.

Kilodavis, C. (2011) *My Princess Boy*. New York: Simon and Schuster.

A young boy who loves to wear dresses is totally accepted by his family.

Kushner, E. (2013) *The Purim Superhero*. Minneapolis, MN: Kar-Ben Publishing.

Nate isn't sure what to dress up as for a Jewish festival and his two dads help him decide.

Merchant, E. (2011) *Dad David, Baba Chris and ME*. London: BAAF.

Ben is adopted by two gay men. The conversations at school help Ben see that children live in all kinds of families.

Newman, L. (2009) *Daddy, Papa and ME*. Berkeley, CA: Tricycle Press.

Newman, L. (2012) *Donovan's Big Day*. Berkeley, CA: Tricycle Press.

Donovan's mums are getting married and as ringbearer, this is a very big day for him!

Newman, L. (2009) *Mommy, Mama and ME*. Berkeley, CA: Tricycle Press.

A small child spends the day with his/her two mothers, and the routines of dressing, bathing and a goodnight kiss are beautifully illustrated.

Oelschlager, V. (2010) *A Tale of Two Daddies*. Akron, OH: Vanita Books.

This story is told through the playground conversation of two children, one of whom has two dads.

Oelschlager, V. (2011) *A Tale of Two Mommies*. Akron, OH: Vanita Books.

An enjoyable story about a little boy with two mothers.

Parr, T. (2010) *The Mommy Book*. New York: Little, Brown and Company.

A bright and colourful book showing that all mothers are different!

Richardson, J. and Parnell, P. (2006) *And Tango Makes Three*. New York: Simon and Schuster Children's Books.

The true story of two male penguins that form a close bond and were found trying to hatch a stone. They are given an egg of their own to raise. They successfully hatch and raise the chick. Tango is the only penguin to have two dads!

Setterington, K. (2004) *Mom and Mum Are Getting Married*. Toronto: Second Story.

Rosie comes home from school to be told that her mums are getting married. Then the planning begins!

Thomas, P. (2012) *This Is My Family: A First Look at Same-Sex Parents*. New York: Barron's Educational Series.

A picture book that shows that all kinds of parents love and care for their children. The book includes notes for parents and teachers, with ideas about how to share the book with children.

Valentine, J. (2004) *One Dad Two Dads Brown Dads Blue Dads*. New York: Alyson Books.

Two children compare their thoughts about their dads in this entertaining and eye-catching book.

Watson, K. (2005) *Spacegirl Pukes*. London: Onlywomen Press.

When Spacegirl starts to feel ill, her two mummies are on hand to help. This book successfully makes having two mummies an incidental part of the story rather than being an issue.

Appendix 2

Useful websites and organisations

http://www.stonewall.org.uk/
Stonewall is a national organisation that campaigns for lesbian, gay and bisexual equality. They have a large education campaign that acts to tackle homophobic bullying and raise awareness. Their resources include the 'Different Families, Same Love' posters. They have recently gained additional funding to widen their educational work to include the early years.

Some of the free resources that are available via the Stonewall website are:

- *Celebrating Difference* – Stonewall's teacher training DVD for primary school staff.

- *Primary Best Practice Guide* – how primary schools are celebrating difference and tackling homophobia.

- Different Families, Same Love – a range of posters, stickers and alternative mother and father cards suitable for special days.

Although some of these are for primary age, we feel that they can be adapted and used by early years practitioners as a basis for good practice.

Stonewall are also an excellent starting point to think of in-house training. There is also the possibility of becoming a Stonewall Champion. In order to do this, the setting needs to send a representative to one of the 'Train the Trainer' sessions that are held across the UK during the year. After the training, the setting becomes part of the ongoing Champions programme and receives support and advice in tackling homophobia and maintaining good practice. Currently this scheme is directed towards primary and secondary schools.

http://www.outforourchildren.org.uk/
Out For Our Children is an organisation run by a group of lesbian mothers who wanted to help nurseries support their families. Their site includes lots of information on resources, training and law. They have produced their own posters and cards. There is a short animated video that would greatly support practitioners to begin to think about this aspect of inclusion. This can be found at http://www.outforourchildren. org.uk/resources/ They also produce a Foundation Stage Pack with lots of ideas for activities, and an extensive book list at http://www. outforourchildren.org.uk/childrens-books/. There are also links to other relevant organisations.

http://www.letterboxlibrary.com/index.html
Letterbox Library is a 31-year-old, not-for-profit, children's bookseller specialising in books which celebrate inclusion, equality and diversity. They are famous for their book selection process and all of the books they stock have been approved by an independent team of reviewers that includes early years and primary teachers, librarians, social workers and children. You can see all of their books on their website and you can search under several relevant themes, including 'LGBT' and 'Families'.

http://mymotherfullfamily.wordpress.com/
Blog written by Shoshana Davidson, a woman in her mid-twenties who grew up with her two mothers and younger brother. She regularly updates the blog with new posts about all aspects of her life and her thoughts about growing up with LGBT+ parents.

http://www.persona-doll-training.org/ukhome.html
Website with information about all aspects of working with Persona Dolls. Includes information about training and also provides case studies and stories. The dolls can be ordered through the site.

http://www.eenet.org.uk/resources/docs/Index%20EY%20English.pdf
This is a link to a pdf of the Index for Inclusion mentioned in Chapter 5. All the questionnaires and tick lists are included.

http://www.wearefamilymagazine.co.uk/index.php
We Are Family is a magazine by and for the LGBT community. All aspects of family life are covered, including LGBT parenting and grandparenting, supporting an LGBT child and issues to do with education.

http://www.baaf.org.uk/info/lgbt
The British Association for Adoption and Fostering provide a wealth of information about lesbian and gay fosterers and adopters. This includes books for adults and children. The two picture books they produce (Hedi Argent's *Josh and Jaz Have Three Mums* and Ed Merchant's *Dad David, Baba Chris and ME*) would be an asset to any early years setting (full details given in Appendix 1).

http://twolivesbooks.wordpress.com/
This publisher specialises in publishing books for children with LGBTQ parents.

http://www.theguardian.com/teacher-network/teacher-blog/2014/oct/29/transgender-supporting-students-school-lgbt
An interesting article that discusses the need for those working in education to have training in how to support children who identify as LGBT.

http://lesbiangayparents.ning.com/
This is a site for LGBT parents and for those considering parenthood. It is packed full of information that settings might find useful.

https://www.newfamilysocial.org.uk/
New Family Social is a site for LGBT adoptive and foster families. There are lots of helpful and informative resources available.

http://www.rainbowfam.co.uk/
This is a useful site for LGBT parents and others interested in the issues, as it has links to literature and other resources.

http://www.rainbowfamilies.org.uk/
Although this group is based in Brighton and Hove, there is some useful information and links on their website.

http://www.huffingtonpost.co.uk/shaun-dellenty/lgbt-teachers_b_6077366.html
This interesting article shows the importance of LGBT practitioners being able to be 'out' at work. While the article focuses on the experience of a teacher in a school, the issues apply equally to early years practitioners.

Further reading

Atkinson, E. and DePalma, R. (2010) *Undoing Homophobia in Primary Schools*. Stoke on Trent: Trentham Books.

Although this project mainly focused on primary schools there is a section on the early years. The project explored the ways in which teachers have challenged the silences in education around sexuality and gender.

Brown, B. (2007) *Unlearning Discrimination in the Early Years*, Staffordshire: Trentham Books.

While this book doesn't give much attention to issues of sexuality, it is a central text in how to challenge discrimination in the early years and much of the discussion applies equally to all forms of discrimination.

Davies, L. (2010) *Out For Our Children. Foundation Stage Pack*, London, Out For Our Children.

This is a fantastic resource for all early years settings and reception classes. There are lots of activity ideas for building on books that show families with LGBT parents and for using Persona Dolls to introduce family diversity to groups of children.

Epstein, B. (2013) *Are the Kids All Right?* London: HammerOn Press.

This book explores children's literature that includes an LGBT theme. There is an extensive list of books for all age groups.

Guasp, A. (2010) *Different Families. The Experiences of Children with Lesbian and Gay Parents*. London: Stonewall/Centre for Family Research.

This report from Stonewall focuses on the experiences of families with lesbian and gay parents. It is also available as a download from their website.

Kane, E. (2013) *Rethinking Gender and Sexuality in Childhood.* London: Bloomsbury.

This book explores gender and sexuality in children's lives and is written in a very clear and accessible style. There are also activities that would be helpful for staff groups to explore.

Robinson, K. (2002) Making the Invisible Visible: Gay and Lesbian Issues in Early Childhood Education. *Contemporary Issues in Early Childhood,* 3(3): 414–434.

This article argues that issues of sexuality should be part of the anti-bias approach in early years.

Wolpert, E. (2005) *Start Seeing Diversity. The Basic Guide to an Anti-Bias Classroom,* St Paul, MN: Redleaf Press.

One of the few books on diversity in the early years that includes a section on sexuality. This would be a useful starting point for those wanting to explore the issues further.

Index

Early Years Foundation Stage (EYFS)
14, 39–40, 70, 105; and inclusive
practice 69–70; inspection
process 105–7; reports 107–9
edited lives 99–100, 121
education, of children 40–1
Education and Inspection Act 2006
70
empathy 77, 104, 114–15
Employment Equality (Sexual
Orientation) Act 2003 44
England 44
environment 37, 73, 81, 99–100,
124; home 125; importance of
14, 103; learning 27, 73–4;
offensive 32, 35; supportive and
inclusive 2, 7, 61, 89, 95–7, 120;
traditional 9
equal opportunities 40; and EYFS 70
equality 27; current legislative
background 31–2; good practice
7–8, 30, 40, 65, 95, 103, 106,
112, 124; resourcing for 103–5;
successful approach to 75
Equality Act 2010 32–3, 70; ACAS
guide to 33; protected
characteristics under 33
Equality Act (Sexual Orientation)
Regulations 2007 44
events, marking of 85
exclusion: minimal 67; social 23
experience: childhood 79, 102, 106–
8, 111–12, 115–16, 118, 123; of
discrimination 25; of life 14, 49;
of marriage 8; pooling of 86;
practitioners' 5, 9, 92; provision
of 41

families 1, 6; in books 109–10;
definition of 48–9; different types
of 49, 74, 78, 85; environment of
2; and the Equality Act 34;

extended 58–9; finding a
narrative for 62; good practice
with 70–3; hierarchy of 26; and
homophobia 53–5; with
intersectionality 56–8; intricate
structures of 112; with LGBT
parents 49–59, 120; life events in
49; living apart 48; multi-adult
51–2; 'normal' 62; practice with
7, 67–87; 'proper' 54; settling-in
of 75; support of 2; telling stories
about 61–4; toy sets representing
115–17; working with 120
family hierarchy 26
fathers, children with two 49, 81, 96,
126
fostering 55–8

gay: definition of 18–19; identifying
as 107; illegality of 42, 44;
meaning of 3; as mental illness
39; as a negative expression 5,
25, 46, 79, 121; stereotypes 21,
93
gay families see families, with LGBT
parents
gay homes/households see families,
with LGBT parents
gay people 118; criminalisation of
42, 44; and paedophilia 91, 96;
valued 84
gender 3–4, 90–2; assigned 19;
choice 121; identity 19; internal
sense of 19; questions about 106;
reassignment as protected
characteristic 33; roles 24;
stereotypes 24
good practice see practice, good
Graham, Bob 110
group belonging, and othering 20
groups, minority 22
guidance 31

sexism 22
sexual acts: age of consent for
11–12, 44; legalisation of 44
sexual choices, conversations
about 2
sexual identity 107
Sexual Offences (Amendment) Act
2000 44
sexual orientation 18–19; as
protected characteristic 33
sexual preference, changeability
of 2
sexuality: of children 3; choice of 2;
development of 2; exploration of
39; and family support 57;
flexibility in 24; fluidity of 19;
and LGBT books 110; play as
indicator of 111–14; questions
about 2–3, 106; and sex 1, 95–6,
121; sharing of status 2; talking
about 99
shared parental leave 38
small world toys 115–17
social exclusion 23
society: binary outlook of 3; tolerant
26
socio-cultural theory 14
sociology of childhood 13–14
Somalia 42
speaking, and equalities practice 8
special needs 5
staff: assumptions exercise for 98;
childhood experiences of 79–80;
environment of 2; and the
Equality Act 34; ethos of 122; gay
71; LGBT 7, 88–101, 120;
meetings of 75; and multi-adult
families 51–2; parental responses
to 18; personal details of 97–8;
professional image of 99–100; as
role models 74; sexuality status of
2, 99; sharing personal

information by 99–100; support
of 2; training of 4, 52, 75, 92,
95–7
stereotypes 6, 20–2, 27, 72, 126;
avoidance of 74; cultural 112;
gender 24; of men in early years
care 90–1; and role-play 18
Stonewall 2, 133–4; as language and
terms resource 4–5; legal
expertise of 30; research by 24–5;
and Section 28 44; training by 95;
website of 133
suicide 125
Sure Start programme 124
surrogacy 53

teams 88, 113, 122
terminology, of LGBT parent families
49
terms 4–5; definition of 18–26
Thatcher, Margaret 44
Tilly's at Home Holiday 110
tolerance 26–7
toys 3, 52, 81, 102, 113; small world
115–17
trainers: approved 95; specialist
4
training 1, 4, 52, 75, 80, 92, 122; by
Stonewall 133; equality 74, 104;
lack of 46; refusal of 37; of staff 7,
9, 52, 75, 82, 94–7, 115;
standoffs in 96
trans community 19
transgender: definition of 18–19; as
mental illness 39
transgender people 5, 112;
discussing childhood by 100;
irrationality towards 23; sexual
choices of 2
transman 19
transphobia 23, 25, 27
transwoman 19

UNICEF (United Nations Children's Fund) 41–3
United Kingdom (UK), legislation in 43–5
United Nations (UN): *Convention on the Rights of the Child* 11, 41–3, 70, 122; Article 2 (Non-discrimination) 42; Article 14 (Freedom of thought, conscience and religion) 43
United States of America (USA) 42, 45
unmarried couples, and adoption 55

vision statements 1, 97
Vygotsky, Lev Semionovich 14

Wales 44
We Are Family, website 135
websites, useful 133–6 Appendix 2
West Sussex County Council, and adoption 56
wider community 58–9
Wolfenden Report 44
women, characterisation of 3
workplace: being 'out' in 97; discrimination in 44
World Health Organization (WHO) 39
wrong body, feelings of 3

young adult (YA) fiction 111

Zone of Proximal Development (ZPD) 14